Stringing
Style 2

Stringing
Style2

*50 More Designs
for Beaded Jewelry*

JEAN CAMPBELL

INTERWEAVE PRESS
www.interweave.com

Acknowledgments

Thanks to all the hardy folks at Interweave Press for their work on this book, especially editor (and superstar jewelry designer) Jamie Hogsett, who has stamped her own style on *Beadwork Presents Stringing,* taking it from a one-time experiment to an influential jewelry style quarterly magazine. To Marlene Blessing, Danielle Fox, and Dustin Wedekind for going the extra mile, not only with putting out those extra special issues, but also contributing such fabulous work to its pages; and to Rebecca Campbell, who, in addition to contributing some pretty stellar stringing style herself, is also a pretty wonderful book editor.

Of course this book wouldn't be possible without the creative contributions of all the designers listed within. Their work dazzles and delights while at the same time pushes beading and jewelry design into the artistic realm. And that's no small feat.

And to my gang on Rosemary Road, who cheer when new deadlines are assigned and when old ones are met.

Photography, Joe Coca
Design, Paulette Livers

Photography, text, and illustrations © 2007 Interweave Press LLC

Interweave Press LLC
201 East Fourth Street
Loveland, Colorado 80537 USA
www.interweave.com

Printed in China by C & C Offset Printing Co., Ltd.

Library of Congress Cataloging-in-Publication Data

Stringing style 2 : 50 more designs for beaded jewelry / Jean Campbell, editor.
    p. cm.
 Includes index.
 ISBN-13: 978-1-59668-036-4 (pbk.)
 ISBN-10: 1-59668-036-9 (pbk.)
 1. Beadwork. 2. Jewelry making. I. Campbell, Jean, 1964-
 TT860.S783 2007
 745.594'2--dc22

                          2006020652

10 9 8 7 6 5 4 3 2 1

Contents

Introduction 7

Stringing 101 8

Bracelet Bonanza 20

Earring Euphoria 24

The Projects

Introduction

They glisten, sparkle, and shine, but can also be matte, bumpy, or opaque. They have solid, striped, polka-dotted, or psychedelic patterns. They're round, square, oval, or shaped like talons, spikes, or paddles. They can be machine or handmade, either locally or far away. Some you can find anywhere, and others you'll kick yourself for not snatching up when you had the chance. And they are just like potato chips—you can't stop at just one.

If you've been flipping through this book, it's no secret what I'm writing about: beautiful, bountiful, BEADS! Their sheer numbers and types continue to stupefy even an old bead hound like me, and I still feel a silly thrill every time I encounter a bead I've never seen before.

It's not hard to imagine their potential once you start stringing these little gems together. When I started making my own beaded jewelry, all my notions of what jewelry is (something that you might see in a Sunday newspaper ad) were smashed to bits. My eyes became wide open to what jewelry can be, and how beading my own jewelry meant a treasure trove of creative possibilities. . . . Make a necklace with silk and wire? Yes! A bracelet with glass and embroidery floss? Of course! By finding the most unique combination of materials, bead types, and colors, I found that stringing beads can flourish into the artistic realm, and once I wore my designs my creative spirit really shined through.

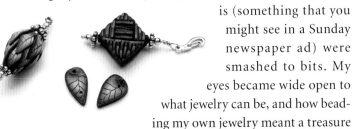

Whether you like it or not, you've already experienced a leap into that artistic realm by simply opening this book. It's impossible to not be creatively inspired by such beauty! The stunning projects you see—all by top jewelry designers—are the cream-of-the-crop from the most recent *Beadwork Magazine Presents Stringing* issues plus twelve brand-new designs. The projects range from bold to delicate, sophisticated to fanciful. Some are perfect to wear at the office, some at a gala opening event. And all, hopefully, will give you the itch to dive deeper into beading.

The next best thing to all the eye candy in this book is that it includes all the things you need to know to make what you see. The first step in getting started is to head to your favorite bead store. Ask one of the shop staff to help you out, using the project's materials list as a shopping list. Also check out the resource list at the bottom of each project. It can help you locate some of those harder-to-find items. Again, your local bead shop should be able to help you here, especially with those vendors who are wholesale only—most shops are happy to make orders for you.

Once you get home with your materials, cozy up to the worktable. It's probably best to read the comprehensive basics section starting on page 8, Stringing 101, before you actually start beading. For those of you who are new beaders, it'll give you a crash course in all the materials, tools, and techniques used in the book's projects. (It can also serve as a refresher to all you seasoned beaders.) Once you've got all that information under your belt, simply follow the project's clear step-by-step instructions, and get stringing!

My hope is that this book not only helps you become passionate about beading but also acts as a springboard for you to start creating your own designs. Use the projects as a starting point and try your hand at incorporating other bead colors and types to make a piece that fits your style. Before you know it, you'll be designing like the pros.

Happy beading,

Jean Campbell

Stringing 101

Whether you're new to beading or have been doing it for years, it's a good idea to check your knowledge before beginning any project. The following section is your personal crash course in bead stringing. It covers all the materials, tools, and techniques you'll use to make the projects in this book and can help you gain the confidence to get designing your own fabulous jewelry.

BEADS

There is a myriad of beads in the bead world! Different shapes, styles, colors, and they come from every country and in just about every type of material. There isn't room here to give a full listing of what's available out there, but the following is a good overview of the types of beads you'll be using in this book.

Bone and horn beads are handmade beads that usually come from Indonesia and the Philippines; they're created from the bone or horns of working animals such as goats, camels, and cattle. Initially white, bone beads can be dyed any color.

Bugle beads are made by cutting a long, thin, hollow glass tube (generally called a "cane") into smaller lengths. These long, thin beads are sized by number—1, 2, 3, and 5. Use durable thread, beading wire, or a seed bead between bugle beads because their sharp edges can cut the thread or wire.

Ceramic beads are handmade clay beads that have been fired at a high temperature. The beads can be glazed, resulting in a shiny finish and many colors, or left natural, resulting in a matte brown finish.

Charms are small, usually flat, pieces of metal that have a loop on the top through which you may string. Charms usually have a figurative design or carry a message and are a fun addition to strung designs.

Crystal beads most often come from the Swarovski company in Austria. Crisp facets and a clean finish on these leaded glass beads create their brilliant sparkle. Crystals come in several shapes (round, bicone, drop, and cubes) and nearly one hundred colors. Use durable beading wire with crystal beads because their sharp edges can cause extra wear.

 Czech pressed-glass beads are colorful beads from the Czech Republic made by pressing glass into a variety of molds. The beads are also called Czech glass and come in special shapes that range from simple rounds, ovals, and squares to leaves, flowers, animals, and just about any other shape you desire.

Dichroic glass beads are handmade glass beads made with a special kind of glass that is thinly layered with several different metals that produce different colors depending on how the light reflects off of it.

 Enamel beads are metal (usually brass or copper) beads that have been painted or baked with enamel, which gives them a glossy, smooth, colorful surface.

Fire-polished beads are Czech glass beads that start as rounds and are then hand or machine faceted to catch the light. These beads come in every color imaginable and are available with several different added surface finishes that create extra sparkle.

Fused glass beads are artistic handmade beads created with pieces of glass that have been fused together in a kiln. A mandrel is inserted between the pieces before they are melted to create a hole for beading.

Lampworked beads are artistic handmade beads created with hot glass spun onto a mandrel over a flame. Since

some lampworked beads can be exceptionally heavy, use stringing materials appropriate for their weight.

Metal beads vary in type of metal, shape, and size, and they're a great accent for glass and stone beads.

 Bali silver beads are handmade sterling silver beads made in Bali, Indonesia.

Brass beads are made with a mix of copper and zinc and have a dull golden color. Handmade African brass beads are known for their ornate designs and are created using a traditional ancient lost wax technique.

Gold-filled beads are those in which 1/10 of 12k gold is applied to the surface of brass or another base metal. The resulting bead is very strong.

Pewter beads are a dull silver color and are a less expensive alternative to other metal beads. Make sure the pewter is lead free.

PMC (precious metal clay) beads are handmade from a claylike substance that can be rolled, formed, and treated like clay; when fired, PMC becomes 99.9 percent fine silver.

Silver and 18k gold-plated beads are created by an electroplating process. A very thin layer of silver or gold is applied to another type of metal like brass or copper.

 *Sterling silver beads* are a mix of silver and copper. To be sold legally as sterling, the percentages must be 92.5 percent pure silver and 7.5 percent copper. While some people have allergic skin reactions when wearing less pure metal jewelry, most can wear sterling silver jewelry without such reactions.

Thai silver beads are handmade in Thailand by the Karen hill tribe, who use old car parts and other found objects as tools to make their beads. Thai silver is 99.5 to 99.9 percent fine silver.

Vermeil (pronounced vehr-MAY) beads are made of sterling silver electroplated with gold.

Pearl beads come in several types and qualities. The projects in this book use both cultured freshwater and Swarovski crystal pearls.

Freshwater pearls are cultured in inland lakes and rivers. The pearls are real pearls, as they are collected from oysters, but the irritant that formed the pearl was manually inserted. Therefore, they come in all sizes and shapes.

Crystal pearl beads are new from Swarovski. They are crystals that have been coated with a pearl-like substance. Because crystal is the core of these pearls, they have the same weight as real pearls, a benefit over other imitation pearls.

Polymer clay beads are colorful handmade plasticine (a claylike substance made of synthetic materials) beads that are fired at low temperatures. Polymer clay is often used to make colorful pendants in all sorts of patterns, shapes, and sizes.

Porcelain beads are made from a combination of clay, silica, and feldspar that is fired at a very high temperature (2650°). The result is a hard, nonporous, translucent material similar to glass.

Seed beads are tiny pieces of a thin, long glass cane that are melted slightly or tumbled to round the edges. Seed beads come in several different finishes, such as iridescent, matte, satin, silver-lined, and transparent.

Cylinder beads (brand names: Delicas, Tohos, and Magnificas), are perfectly cylindrical beads with thin walls and large holes. They come in two sizes—regular and large, which approximate a size 11° seed bead and a size 8° seed bead.

Czech seed beads come on hanks, are shaped like tiny donuts, and are slightly irregular. They are sized from 20° to 6° (the smaller the number, the larger the bead). Charlottes are size 13° beads with a facet that makes them sparkle.

Japanese seed beads are sold in tubes or by the kilo and are shaped more like cylinders, giving them larger holes. They come in 6°, 8°, 11°, and 14/15° sizes (the smaller the number, the larger the bead). The degree mark next to the size is called an "ought," and is a traditional beading term/symbol; its origin is obscure.

Semiprecious stone beads, are naturally made by the earth or sea creatures, and are available in hundreds of varieties. They come in all sizes and shapes, but generally they are polished and faceted, donut-shaped, rough-cut, or chips. These beads are usually heavy, so use a strong beading wire to string them. More than two dozen different stones are

used in the projects in this book: agate, akynite, amazonite, amber, amethyst, aventurine, carnelian, chalcedony, citrine, fluorite, garnet, jade, jasper, kyanite, labradorite, moukaite, moonstone, onyx, opal, peridot, prehnite, pyrite, quartz, ruby, serpentine, topaz, tourmaline, turquoise, and unakite.

Shell beads are created from natural shells. Beads made from the iridescent substance formed in mollusk shells are marketed as mother-of-pearl beads.

Silk beads are made from rolled pieces of organic silk fabric.

Vintage beads are any type of bead from the late nineteenth to mid-twentieth century that is no longer being manufactured.

Millimeter Size Chart

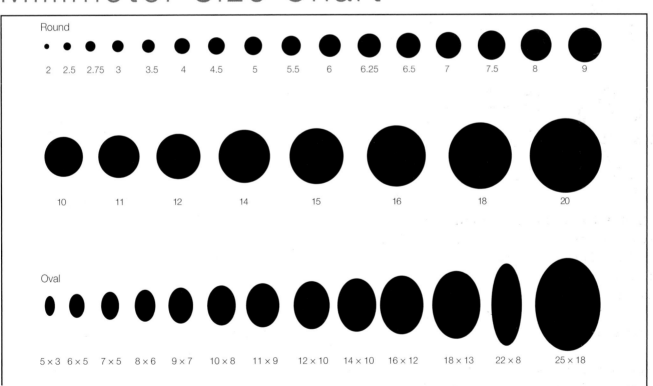

Round

2   2.5   2.75   3   3.5   4   4.5   5   5.5   6   6.25   6.5   7   7.5   8   9

10   11   12   14   15   16   18   20

Oval

5 × 3   6 × 5   7 × 5   8 × 6   9 × 7   10 × 8   11 × 9   12 × 10   14 × 10   16 × 12   18 × 13   22 × 8   25 × 18

Bead Shapes

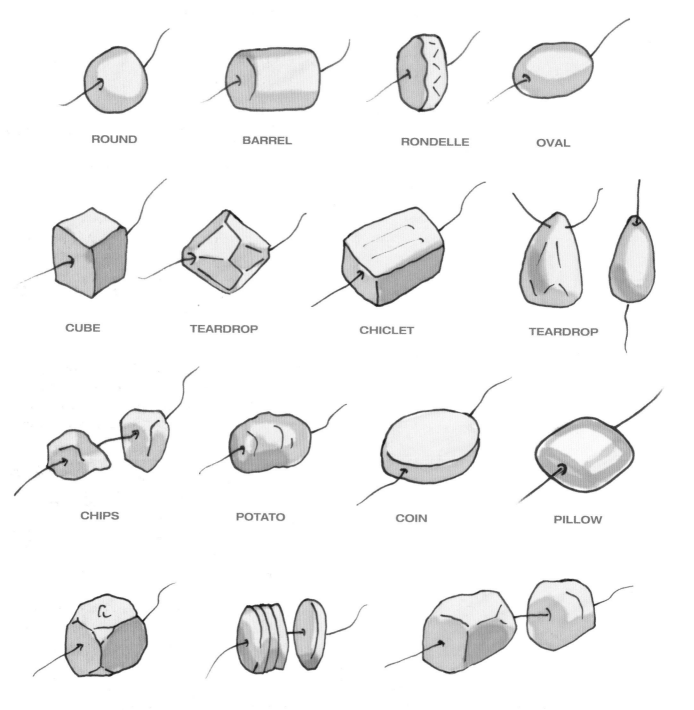

ROUND   BARREL   RONDELLE   OVAL

CUBE   TEARDROP   CHICLET   TEARDROP

CHIPS   POTATO   COIN   PILLOW

CORNERLESS CUBE   HEISHI   NUGGETS

FINDINGS

If you need to connect, link, or secure your stringing designs, chances are you'll be using a finding. Like beads, there are thousands of types, but this short list should give you all the information you'll need for now.

Chain is links of soldered metal loops that act as a base for many jewelry projects. Connect beads and clasps to this finding with jump rings, split rings, or wirework.

Clasps connect the ends of necklaces or bracelets. Some have one loop for single-strand jewelry, others have two or more loops for multistranded pieces.

Box clasps are shaped like a rectangular, square, or circular box on one end and have a bent metal tab on the other end that snaps into the box under its own tension. Many are decorated with beautiful designs and inlaid stones.

Buttons with shanks are a great option for clasps and can also be incorporated into pieces as a focal point or design element.

Hook-and-eye clasps are comprised of a J-shaped side and a loop side that hook into each other. This clasp requires tension to keep it closed, so it's best used with necklaces that have some weight.

Lobster and spring-ring clasps have levers that open an internal spring after which they snap back shut. Secure these clasps to jump rings at the other end of the jewelry.

S-hooks are made up of an S-shaped wire permanently attached to a jump ring on one side; the S closes through a second jump ring on the other end of the piece. This clasp, like the hook and eye, depends on tension to keep it closed.

Toggle clasps are made up of a bar on one side and a ring on the other. A good toggle clasp will not come apart on its own because the bar is long enough so that it must be turned and manually passed through the ring.

Tube clasps are usually multistranded and are made up of two tube shapes, one slightly larger than the other. The large tube is hollow. The smaller tube has a wire that snaps the larger half into place once they are slid together.

Cones cover the end of multistrand pieces to make a clean finish. The best way to use a cone is to attach the multiple strands to an eye pin, pass the eye pin through the cone from the inside out and make a wrapped loop to secure it.

Connectors act as a transition finding between a single strand and multiple strands on a strung piece. Crimp beading wire or tie threads directly to the loops on this finding.

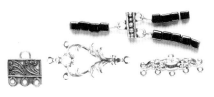

Crimp beads and tubes

help to secure beading wire to clasps and connectors or wherever you need to make a connection. With a preferred size of wire they can hold several strands of wire and look nice. Check on the websites of wire manufacturers to see which crimp tubes work best with a preferred size of wire. See page 17 for instructions on how to use these findings.

Tornado crimps are a new product that work best when flattened with chain- or flat-nose pliers. Their curved design adds an aesthetic element to a piece of jewelry.

Crimp covers are shiny pieces of sterling silver or gold-filled metal that wrap around crimp tubes with the help of crimping pliers. They look like round beads and are a great design element.

Eye pins are straight pieces of wire with a loop on one end.

Head pins are straight pieces of wire with a small stopper at one end that are often used for making earrings or other dangles.

Jump rings are small circles of wire used to connect pieces of beadwork. Most jump rings have a seam where you can open them, but soldered jump rings are closed shut. To open a nonsoldered jump ring, bend the ends away from each other laterally; do not pull the ends apart.

Split rings are shaped like tiny key rings. They are really doubled-up jump rings that create a secure attachment because they don't pull open.

STRINGING MATERIALS

They usually aren't the show stoppers on a strung piece of jewelry, but they provide an important backbone for the beads and findings that are! Make sure to use the highest-quality stringing materials—it will ensure your beautiful creations will stay that way for years to come.

Beading wire (brand names Accuflex, Acculon, Beadalon, Soft Flex) is a very flexible nylon-coated multistrand steel wire available in diameters from .012 to .021. The higher the diameter, the more strands of wire are included in the nylon coating and the more strands, the stronger and more flexible the wire. Use wire cutters to cut this stringing material and secure it using crimp tubes and crimping pliers.

Embroidery floss is made up of strong, 100% cotton thread. The floss is made up of six strands of the thread twisted together; the strands can be used together or apart. It comes in an incredible array of colors and can be cut with a scissors.

Fishing lines (brand names Dandy Line, Fireline, and PowerPro) are fine, no-stretch braided cords that are also used for fishing. They have great strength (10–20 pound test), are very thin (.006 diameter), can be knotted, and come in three colors—moss green, gray, and white. Because of the angle of their blades, children's Fiskars cut these materials better than other scissors.

Leather cord is a round, smooth cord that comes in a variety of colors, can be knotted, and is best used for wide-holed, large beads.

Silk thread and cord come in a variety of colors and widths. They are sold in 24" (61 cm) lengths, by the spool, or on a card (often with a built-in needle). The thin thread is the best choice for stringing pearls, and the wider cord works well for knotting techniques. Prestretch thread and cord (pull back and forth several times) before you use it.

Sinew is traditionally made from the tendons of working animals. Today sinew is made of fine synthetic fibers held together with wax. It is a strong cord often used to string trade beads.

Suede cord is a strip of leather with a napped surface or Ultrasuede (simulated suede). It works well for wide-holed beads or as an embellishment.

Sterling silver wire is the best choice for wirework (for this book's simple stringing purposes, wirework means creating wire loops for things like dangles or earrings). It is relatively soft, so it's easily manipulated but has good memory. Cut this material with wire cutters.

TOOLS

When setting up a bead stringing work station, one great benefit is that you don't need many tools to get started. The ones you do need, however, are very important, so make sure to purchase the best tools you can afford.

Alligator clips and Bead Stoppers are fasteners that keep your beads from slipping off the end of your material while you are still working on a project. Especially useful with beading wire, these helpers are great when making a multistranded piece.

Chain-nose pliers have flat, tapered jaws that come to a point. They work well for pulling beading wire tight and for wrapping wire.

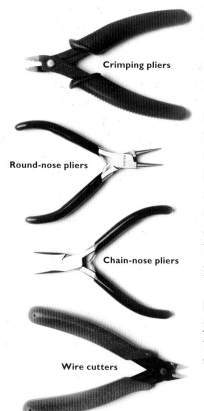

Crimping pliers

Round-nose pliers

Chain-nose pliers

Wire cutters

Crimping pliers squeeze and secure a crimp tube onto beading wire. (See instructions about how to crimp on page 17.)

Design layout boards are boards covered in a flocked material with grooves for laying out necklaces and little slots for keeping beads in one spot. Available in many different varieties, the multistrand boards are ideal for making perfect graduated strands.

Flat-nose pliers have flat jaws and are not tapered. Use them for pulling beading wire tight and to wrap wire.

Hypo Cement is a strong, clear, adhesive glue ("watchmakers glue") that comes with a pinpoint applicator. It works well to secure knots but can also stabilize bead placement in a strung design.

Round-nose pliers have round, tapered jaws that come to a point. Use these pliers to make simple loops and to do wrapping wire.

Vellux mats are small squares of a nonpilling, fuzzy fabric. They are used to keep beads from rolling off the work surface.

Wire cutters have sharp jaws with which to cut beading wire, head pins, eye pins, and other soft wire.

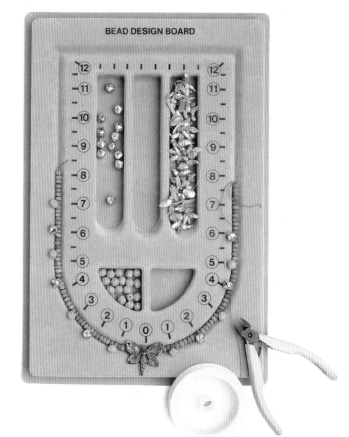

BEAD DESIGN BOARD

CRIMPING

Crimping is a technique that connects beading wire to a finding using a special type of small, hollow metal tube or bead (called "crimp tubes," or "crimp beads"). This professional-looking way to finish your pieces is used on just about every project in this book, but it's not the easiest technique to master. It's best to do a few practice runs using scrap wire before you need to crimp the real deal.

Step 1: String a crimp tube on the beading wire.

Step 2: Pass through the clasp or connector.

Step 3: Pass back through the crimp tube.

Step 4: Snug the crimp tube close to the closure, leaving enough wire space for the clasp to move around freely. (If the wire is pulled too tightly around the clasp, the nylon coating can wear away and eventually break).

Step 5: Spread the two wires so they line each side of the tube, making sure they do not cross in the middle of the tube. Use the first notch on the crimping pliers (round on one jaw, dipped on the other) to squeeze the crimp tube shut, placing one wire on each side of the crimp.

Step 6: Turn the tube onto its side and use the second notch on the crimping pliers (rounded on both jaws) to shape the tube into a tight cylinder. Make gentle squeezes around the tube for perfect rounding.

Step 7: Trim the tail wire close to the tube.

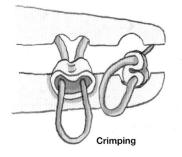

Crimping

Making button and seed bead loop clasps

This homemade clasp is an alternative to its metal counterparts. The design is particularly effective when you wish to work a special button or large bead into the final design, and it often gives the overall piece more unity, especially if you use colors and bead types that you are going to use in the necklace or bracelet.

General instructions are given here to show how to make the clasp, but you may need to modify the number of seed beads to tailor the clasp to your specific button or large bead.

Step 1: Use a shank button to make an anchor for the clasp. To start, measure enough beading wire to complete a one-stranded necklace or bracelet. String 1 crimp tube and the button. Pass back through the crimp tube.

You can also use a bead (9mm or larger) to act as the anchor for your clasp. To begin this technique, measure enough beading wire to complete a one-stranded necklace or bracelet. String 1 crimp tube, the large bead, and 1–3 seed beads. Pass back through the large bead and the crimp tube and crimp.

Step 2: String enough seed beads so that as you lay the strand across the back of the shank button, the end reaches the edge of the button. If you are using a large bead as the anchor, string 1–5 seed beads.

Step 3: String the beads for the body of the necklace or bracelet.

Step 4: String 3 seed beads and 1 crimp tube. String enough seed beads so that when you pass back through the crimp tube the loop slides snugly over the button or large bead. Remove or add seed beads as necessary, pass back through the crimp tube, snug all the beads, and crimp.

KNOTTING

If you're working with a stringing material other than beading wire, you'll need to know how to tie good, strong knots. The following describes those you'll need to know to work the projects in this book.

Lark's head knots are great for securing one piece of material to another piece, like a cord to a donut.
Step 1: Fold the stringing material in half.
Step 2: Pass the fold through the donut.
Step 3: Pull the ends through the loop created in Step 2 and tighten.

The overhand knot is the basic knot for tying off thread.
Step 1: Make a loop with the stringing material.
Step 2: Pass the cord that lies behind the loop over the front cord and through the loop. Pull tight.

Square knots are the classic sturdy knot suitable for most stringing materials.
Step 1: Make an overhand knot, passing the right end over the left end.
Step 2: Make another overhand knot, this time passing the left end over the right end. Pull tight.

WIREWORKING

When you're stringing beads onto metal wire, the following wire techniques are very important to learn. Practice the techniques using scrap wire so you'll have beautiful, clean results on your final piece.

Simple loops turn a piece of wire into a semisecure connector for jump rings or other closures. They are most often used to finish dangles for jewelry or to make rosary chains. Make a double loop (a more secure loop) by turning the round-nose pliers twice to make two loops side by side.
Step 1: Use flat-nose pliers to make a 90° bend at least ½" (1.3 cm) from the end of the wire.

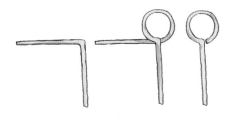

Step 2: Use round-nose pliers to grasp the wire after the bend; roll the pliers toward the bend, but not past it.
Step 3: Use your thumb to continue the wrap around the nose of the pliers. Trim the wire next to the bend.

Wrapped loops are a very secure way to turn a piece of wire into a connector for jump rings or other closures. They're a bit difficult to master, but practice makes perfect.
Step 1: Make a 90° bend 2" (5 cm) from one end of the wire.
Step 2: Use round-nose pliers to form a simple loop with a tail.
Step 3: Wrap the wire tail tightly down the stem of the wire to create two or three coils. Trim the excess wire.

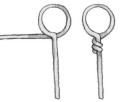

CLASSIC JEWELRY LENGTHS

Bibs are multistrand necklaces that fit below the neckline like a bib. The top strand is shorter than the next strand and so on.

Chokers are necklaces that fit right at the neckline and are 15–16" (38–40.5 cm) in length.

Princess necklaces are 18" (45.5 cm) in length.

Matinee necklaces are 20–26" (51–66 cm) in length.

Opera necklaces are 28–36" (71–91.5 cm) in length.

Rope necklaces are claspless necklaces that fit over the head. They are usually 46" (1.2 m) or longer and are often knotted flapper style.

Lariats are claspless, unconnected beaded ropes that can be knotted, wrapped, looped, or worn in other ways around the neck. They are usually at least 48" (1.3 m) in length.

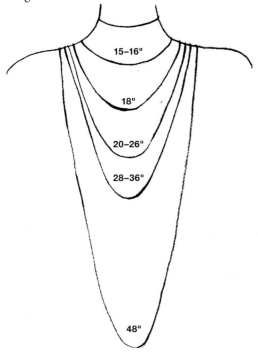

TIPS

- Invest in real metal findings versus plastic painted silver or gold. Not only will your work look classier, the findings will be more durable.

- Invest in good tools. They will make your beading easier, and they will last longer than chintzy counterparts.

- When you buy silver, if the price seems too good to be true, it probably is.

- Keep a small measuring tape and bead-millimeter size chart with you at all times.

- Always buy more beads than you think you will need for a project; this way, you are not only covered for your project, but you'll also begin to develop a bead stash—one of the best things about being a beader!

- Invest in beautiful clasps that complement your pieces. They can often mean the difference between ho-hum and sensational work.

- When you're buying beads, be sure to ask the vendor exactly what type of bead you have bought. This information is quite useful if you ever need to buy more of the same bead.

- Set up your beading surface in a low-lipped tray so that if you spill beads, you won't have to pick them up off the floor.

- Don't jeopardize your most important tool—your eyes! Make sure to bead in good light.

- If you need to adjust a strung piece, and you've left enough extra wire to work with, use sharp, pointed wire cutters to cut the crimp tube free (while you carefully avoid cutting the wire). You can then rework the piece as needed and recrimp.

- Keep a diamond bead reamer on hand to file out tight bead holes.

- Stand back from your work every once in a while. You can catch mistakes and admire your handiwork this way.

- Use inexpensive copper wire to practice wire-working techniques.

- Do not wear your jewelry in the shower or swimming pool. The water will cause the stringing material to weaken or corrode, and it will eventually break.

Bracelet Bonanza

Making a beaded bracelet is about as close to instant gratification as you get! Because they average only seven to eight inches in length, bracelets can be strung quickly and don't use up lots of materials. They are a great way to feature unique beads of which you might only have a few and are certainly a must-make to pair with a necklace or earrings.

To make one, simply attach a 10" piece of beading wire to one half of a clasp using a crimp tube. Then, factoring the length of the clasp into your measurement, string enough beads to fit comfortably around the wrist. Finally, attach the wire to the other half of the clasp using a crimp tube, and trim the wires. You've got yourself a mini-masterpiece! See page 95 for resource information.

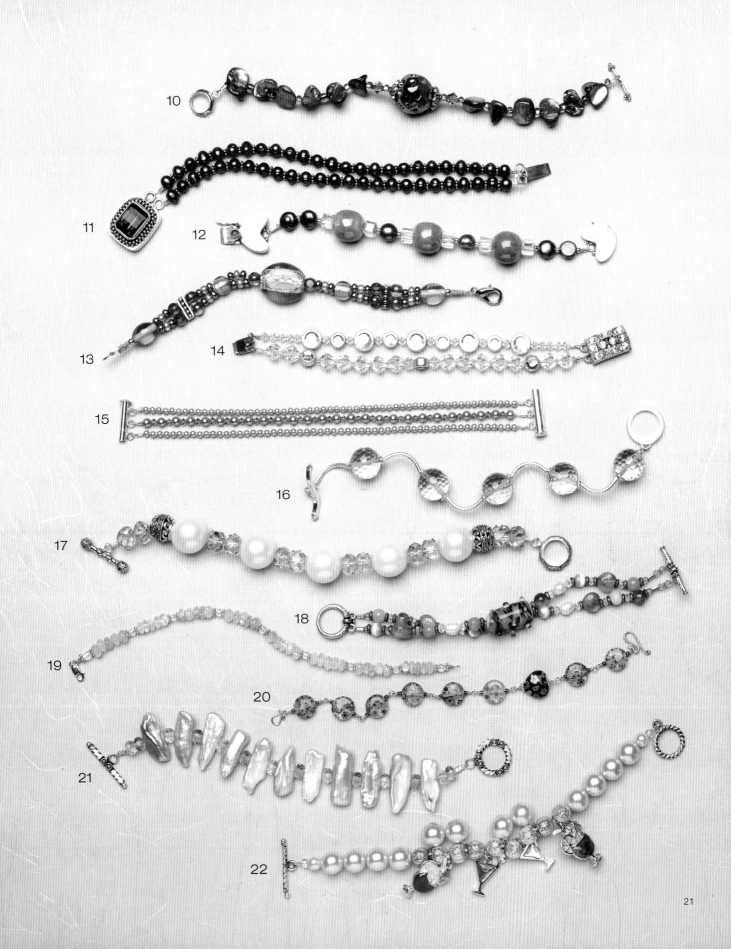

10

11

12

13

14

15

16

17

18

19

20

21

22

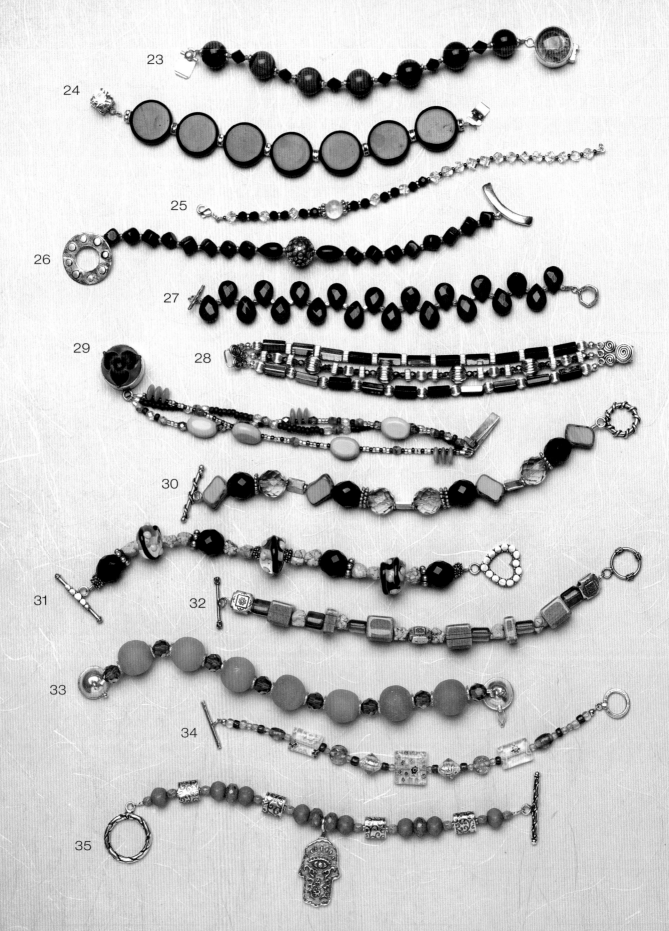

23

24

25

26

27

29

28

30

31

32

33

34

35

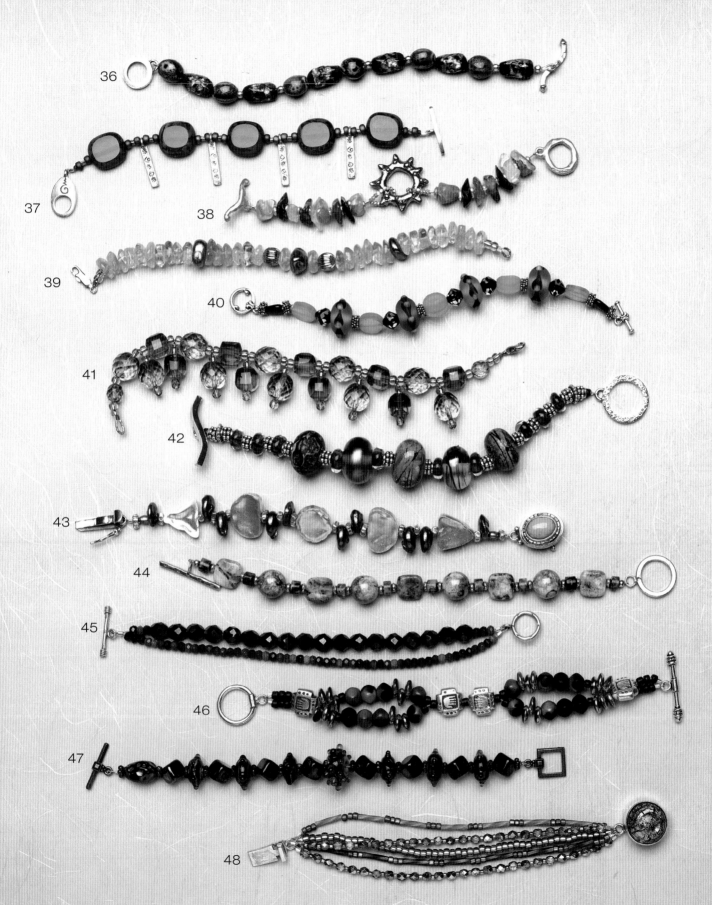

Earring Euphoria

Most women don't leave the house without putting on a pair of earrings first. Making your own is so easy, you'll have no problem making a different pair for every day of the month.

A simple earring is made by first stringing beads onto a head pin and then securing the beads into place with a wrapped loop. Connect the wrapped loop to an earring finding, and you're done! That's the most basic of designs, but as you can see on the following pages, those straightforward directions provide only a glimpse into an earring's design possibilities. See page 95 for resource information.

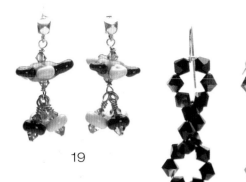

19

20

21

22

23

24

25

26

27

28

29

30

31

32

33

34

35

36

37

38

39

40

41

42

43

44

45

46

47

48

49

50

51

52

53

54

55

56

57

58

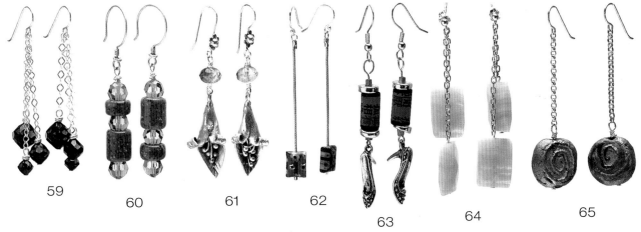

59

60

61

62

63

64

65

66

67

68

69

70

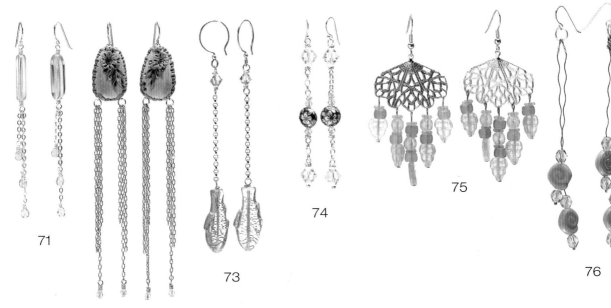

71

72

73

74

75

76

The Projects

Splash

Jaida Kimmerer

J aida made this bracelet to replicate the sparkle of the hot summer sun hitting the water's surface. Graduation in scale and color makes this piece unique and dazzling. The mermaids would be jealous.

MATERIALS

63 clear 3mm Swarovski crystal rounds

46 light azore 4mm Swarovski crystal rounds

36 aquamarine 5mm Swarovski crystal rounds

29 light sapphire 6mm Swarovski crystal rounds

21 sapphire 8mm Swarovski crystal rounds

17 capri blue 10mm Swarovski crystal rounds

12 sterling silver 2mm crimp tubes

12 sterling silver crimp covers

Sterling silver 6-strand slide clasp

60" (152.4 cm) of .014 beading wire

TOOLS

Wire cutters

Crimping pliers

FINISHED SIZE

7¼" (18.4 cm)

Step 1: Attach 10" (25.4 cm) of wire to the first hole of one half of the clasp using a crimp tube. Cover the tube with a crimp cover. String all the clear crystals, 1 crimp tube, and the first hole of the other side of the clasp. Pass back through the tube; crimp and cover.

Step 2: Repeat Step 1 using the second holes of the clasp and all the light azore crystals.

Step 3: Repeat Step 1 using the third holes of the clasp and all the aquamarine crystals.

Step 4: Repeat Step 1 using the fourth holes of the clasp and all the light sapphire crystals.

Step 5: Repeat Step 1 using the fifth holes of the clasp and all the sapphire crystals.

Step 6: Repeat Step 1 using the sixth holes of the clasp and all the capri blue crystals.

RESOURCES

All materials: Fusion Beads.

TIP

Create a slimmer look by using all 3mm rounds and a 3-strand tube clasp, attaching two strands to each loop of the clasp.

Czarina

Jamie Hogsett

With its crown and scepter clasp and long dangly gems, Jamie just needs a coronation invitation as an excuse to wear this necklace.

MATERIALS

18 violet 4mm Swarovski crystal bicones

6 vintage alexandrite 10×14mm glass teardrops

2 vintage alexandrite 12×22mm glass teardrops

3 vintage alexandrite 14×25mm glass teardrops

Sterling silver crown and scepter toggle clasp

6" (15.2 cm) of sterling silver ¼" (.64 cm) link chain

16¼" (41.3 cm) of sterling silver ½" curved-link chain

47" (119.4 cm) of 22-gauge sterling silver wire

TOOLS

Wire cutters

Flat-nose pliers

Round-nose pliers

FINISHED SIZE

17½" (44.5 cm)

Step 1: Use 2" (5.1 cm) of wire to form a wrapped loop that attaches to one half of the clasp. String 1 crystal and form a wrapped loop that attaches to one end of the curved-link chain. Repeat, attaching the other half of the clasp to the other end of the chain.

Step 2: Cut the ¼" (.64 cm) link chain into two 2-link pieces, two 4-link pieces, and one 6-link piece.

Step 3: Use 2" (5.1 cm) of wire to form a wrapped loop that attaches to the center link of the curved link chain. String 1 crystal and form a wrapped loop that attaches to one end of the 6-link chain. Use 3" (7.6 cm) of wire to form a wrapped loop that attaches to the other end of the 6-link chain. String 1 crystal and form a wrapped-loop bail around a 14×25mm teardrop.

Step 4: Use 3" (7.6 cm) of wire to form a wrapped loop that attaches to the next link to the left of the one in the previous step. String 1 crystal and form a wrapped-loop bail around a 10×14mm teardrop.

Step 5: Use 2" (5.1 cm) of wire to form a wrapped loop that attaches to the next link to the left. String 1 crystal and form a wrapped loop that attaches to one end of a 4-link chain. Use 3" (7.6 cm) of wire to form a wrapped loop that attaches to the other end of the 4-link chain. String 1 crystal and form a wrapped-loop bail around a 14×25mm teardrop. Repeat Step 4 for the next link to the left.

Step 6: Use 2" (5.1 cm) of wire to form a wrapped loop that attaches to the next link to the left. String 1 crystal and form a wrapped loop that attaches to one end of a 2-link piece of chain. Use 3" (7.6 cm) of wire to form a wrapped loop that attaches to the other end of the 2-link chain. String 1 crystal and form a wrapped-loop bail around a 12×22mm teardrop. Repeat Step 4 for the next link to the left.

Step 7: Repeat Steps 4–6 for the right half of the necklace.

RESOURCES

Chain and crystals: Fusion Beads. Clasp: Carl Clasmeyer.

Purple Haze

Terry Rhoades

Purple—royal, rich, powerful, sultry, passionate. Vibrant purple turquoise mixed with crystals and silver is perfect for the darker shades of fall.

MATERIALS

14 lavender 6mm Swarovski crystal bicones
8 purple turquoise 12mm squares
23 purple turquoise 12mm tubes
97 sterling silver 3mm cubes
4 sterling silver 15mm frames
2 sterling silver 12mm 2-strand flower spacers
14×30mm etched stone pendant
10×20mm 2-strand box clasp
4 sterling silver 2mm crimp tubes
1 sterling silver head pin
48" (122 cm) of .019 beading wire

TOOLS

Wire cutters
Crimping pliers

FINISHED SIZE

19" (48.3 cm)

Step 1: Use the head pin to string the pendant and form a wrapped loop.

Step 2: Attach 22" (56 cm) of wire to the bottom hole of one half of the clasp using a crimp tube. String 3 cubes, 1 bicone, 1 square, the top hole of a frame, 1 bicone, the bottom hole of the frame, 1 square, 1 bicone, 3 cubes, 1 tube, 1 cube, 1 tube, 1 cube, 1 tube, 3 cubes, 1 bicone, 1 square, the top hole of a frame, 1 bicone, the bottom hole of the frame, 1 square, 1 bicone, 3 cubes, 1 top hole of a spacer, 3 cubes, 1 tube, 7 cubes, 1 tube, 7 cubes, 1 tube, 4 cubes, 1 top hole of the spacer, 3 cubes, 1 bicone, 1 square, the bottom hole of a frame, 1 bicone, the top hole of a frame, 1 square, 1 bicone, 3 cubes, 1 tube, 1 cube, 1 tube, 1 cube, 1 tube, 3 cubes, 1 bicone, 1 square, the bottom hole of a frame, 1 bicone, the top hole of a frame, 1 square, 1 bicone, 3 cubes, 1 crimp tube, and the bottom hole of the other half of the clasp. Pass back through the tube and crimp.

Step 3: Attach 26" (66 cm) of wire to the top hole of one half of the clasp using a crimp tube. String 3 cubes. Pass through the bicone, square, frame, bicone, frame, square, and bicone of the previous strand. String 3 cubes, 1 tube, 1 cube, 1 tube, 1 cube, 1 tube, and 3 cubes. Pass through the bicone, square, frame, bicone, frame, square, and bicone of the previous strand. String 3 cubes, the other hole of the spacer used in Step 2, 1 cube, 1 tube, 3 cubes, 1 tube, 3 cubes, 1 tube, 3 cubes, 1 tube, and 1 bicone.

Step 4: String the pendant and repeat Step 3, reversing the stringing sequence, and attaching the wire to the top hole of the clasp.

RESOURCES

Purple turquoise: Dakota Enterprises. Silver frames and cubes: Singaraja Imports. Silver flower spacers: Scattered Light. Purple pendant: The Moontide Workshop. Box clasp: Bokamo Designs.

Blue Shimmy

Dustin Wedekind

When teardrop beads are strung together they like to swish back and forth on the wire. This movement is reflected in the wire coils of the enamel beads and the curvy shape of the glass pendant.

MATERIALS

14 blue silver-lined AB size 8° seed beads
64 blue AB 8mm glass rondelles
48 blue 7×10mm faceted pearl teardrops
9 blue 5×27mm enameled copper tubes
Sterling silver hook-and-eye clasp
4 sterling silver 2mm crimp tubes
46" (117 cm) of .019 beading wire

TOOLS

Wire cutters
Crimping pliers

FINISHED SIZE

18¼" (46.4 cm) (shortest strand)

Step 1: Attach 22" (56 cm) of wire to one half of the clasp using a crimp tube. String 5 seed beads, 1 rondelle, 1 seed bead, 1 rondelle, 1 seed bead, and 1 rondelle.

Step 2: String 1 tube, 1 rondelle, 1 pearl, and 1 rondelle eight times. String 1 tube. Repeat Step 1, reversing the sequence and using the other half of the clasp.

Step 3: Attach 24" (61 cm) of wire to one half of the clasp using a crimp tube. String 1 rondelle and 1 pearl twenty times. String 1 rondelle, the pendant, and 1 rondelle. String 1 pearl and 1 rondelle twenty times. String 1 crimp tube and the other half of the clasp. Pass back through the tube and crimp.

RESOURCES

Pendant: Crystal Myths/Lewis Wilson. Enamel tubes: Da Beads. Pearls: Lucky Gems & Jewelry (wholesale only). Glass rondelles: Stormcloud Trading.

Surf

Candice Schneider

The rich, smooth look of the mother-of-pearl teardrops paired with the rough yet scintillating tourmaline slices gives this necklace a definite oceanic flavor.

MATERIALS

12 crystal quartz chips
2 amber 6mm rounds
2 crystal AB 8mm Swarovski top-drilled bicones
2 smoky lemon quartz 10×12mm fancy cut diagonally drilled squares
5 watermelon tourmaline top-drilled stone slices in various sizes (10mm –18mm)
60 mother-of-pearl top-drilled flat teardrop beads in various sizes (5×8mm –9×12mm)
1 gray/green 22mm lampworked glass coin
1 jade 35×40mm vertically drilled flat oval pendant
1 sterling silver 8mm open jump ring
1 sterling silver 7mm soldered jump ring
1 sterling silver 3" (7.5 cm) head pin
2 sterling silver crimp covers
2 sterling silver 2mm crimp tubes
32mm sterling silver toggle clasp
11⅞" (30 cm) of sterling silver 6×10mm oval and circle chain
12" (30 cm) of sterling silver 22-gauge wire
17¾" (45 cm) of .014 sterling silver beading wire

TOOLS

Wire cutters
Chain-nose pliers
Round-nose pliers
Crimping pliers
2 Bead Stoppers or tape

FINISHED SIZE

30" (76.2 cm)

Step 3: Attach one end of the beaded strand to the folded end of the chain using a crimp tube. Attach the other end of the beaded strand to the ring half of the clasp. Use crimp covers to hide each crimp tube. Set the necklace aside.

Step 4: Use the head pin to string the pendant. Form a wrapped loop that attaches to the soldered ring already strung on the necklace.

Step 5: Cut 7" (17.5 cm) of the 22-gauge wire. Secure it to the pendant either by passing it through the pendant's hole or by twisting it around the wrapped loop. Wrap the wire around the pendant twice, crisscrossing the wire at some point on the front of the pendant. Secure the wire as before.

Step 6: Cut 5" (12.5 cm) of the 22-gauge wire and form a double simple loop on one end. String 3 teardrops, and the bicones. Secure this piece to the pendant where the wires cross.

RESOURCES

Lampworked bead: Bead Monkey.

Step 1: Use the beading wire to string a random pattern of 8 chips, 45 teardrops, and 2 smoky lemon quartz to cover 8" (20 cm) of the wire. String the soldered jump ring. String a random pattern of 4 chips, 12 teardrops, the lampworked bead, 2 amber, and the stone slices. String 1 crimp tube on each end of the wire. Place stoppers or tape on each end of the strand and set aside.

Step 2: Fold the chain in half and use the open jump ring to attach the loose ends to the bar half of the toggle clasp.

Pinky Tuscadero

Rebecca Campbell

The fire-polished beads added to this design lend just the right touch to complement and accentuate the pink bits in the turquoise focal bead. They provide glint without overpowering the turquoise, a hefty nugget which feels oh, so good against your skin.

MATERIALS
35 sea foam green matte size 11° seed beads
12 teal 3mm faceted glass rounds
48 pink 4×6mm Czech pressed glass drops
24 pink 6mm Czech fire-polished glass bicones
4 teal 10mm glass rounds
1 turquoise 3×3cm nugget
1 sea foam green 1.5cm vintage button
2 sterling silver 2mm crimp tubes
18" (46 cm) of .019 beading wire

TOOLS
Wire cutters
Crimping pliers

FINISHED SIZE
15" (38.1 cm)

Step 1: Attach one end of the wire to the button using a crimp tube.

Step 2: String 5 bicones, 1 teal 10mm round, 1 bicone, 1 teal 10mm round, and 24 glass drops. String one 3mm round and 1 bicone six times.

Step 3: String the turquoise nugget. Repeat Step 2, reversing the stringing sequence.

Step 4: String 1 crimp tube and the seed beads. Pass back through the tube and crimp.

RESOURCES
Seed beads and drops: Fusion Beads.
Turquoise nugget, vintage button, and bicones: Bead Cache.
Glass rounds: Loveland Bead Company.

Parlez-Vous Francais?

Danielle Fox

This simple wireworked necklace features opalescent Swarovski crystals and beautiful handpainted silk beads adorned with French script. Delicate chain connects the brilliant components in this très chic piece.

MATERIALS

8 violet opal 8mm Swarovski crystal rondelles
6 Pacific opal 8mm Swarovski crystal rondelles
2 silk 7×15mm beads
7×25mm silk bead
10" (25.4 cm) of 2mm sterling silver cable chain
24 sterling silver 5mm jump rings
16mm sterling silver lobster clasp
2 sterling silver 3" (8 cm) head pins
20" (51 cm) of 22-gauge sterling silver wire

TOOLS

Wire cutters
Round-nose pliers
Flat-nose pliers

FINISHED SIZE

16½" (42 cm)

Step 1: Use a head pin to string 1 violet opal, one 7×15mm silk bead, and 1 violet opal. Form a wrapped loop to make a dangle. Repeat this step with Pacific opal crystals. Use jump rings to attach a ⅝" (2 cm) piece of chain to one dangle and a ¼" (.64 cm) piece to the other.

Step 2: Cut a 4" (10.2 cm) piece of wire and form a wrapped loop at one end. String 1 violet opal, the 7×25 silk bead, and 1 violet opal. Form a wrapped loop. Use jump rings to attach the two pieces of chain from the previous step to one of the loops.

Step 3: Cut a 2" (5 cm) piece of wire and form a wrapped loop at one end. String 1 crystal and form a wrapped loop. Repeat for each remaining crystal.

Step 4: Use a jump ring to attach the dangle made in Step 2 to a 1" (2.5 cm) piece of chain. Attach the other end of the chain to a Pacific opal link from Step 3 using a jump ring. Alternating crystal colors, continue using jump rings to connect 1" (2.5 cm) pieces of chain to three more crystal links. Connect the chain on the top end of the last link to one half of the clasp. Repeat for the other half of the necklace.

RESOURCES

Silk beads: Sassy Silkies; crystals: Beyond Beadery.

Minnesota Winter

Tina Koyama

O n a chilly winter day in St. Paul, Tina noticed frost shimmering in the corners of windows, and she's captured that effect in the way the clear bugle beads shimmer in this elegant multistrand necklace. Don't worry about making all the strands identical—variety adds to the necklace's charm.

Step 1: Cut a 25" (63.5 cm) length of thread and place a piece of tape 5" (13 cm) from one end. String 1–1½" (2.5–4 cm) of each color in the following order for a total of 15" (38 cm): transparent dark, silver-lined dark, transparent medium, silver-lined medium, pearl-finish pale, clear, bugle beads, clear, pearl-finish pale, silver-lined medium, and transparent medium. Work transitions by alternating colors for 6 beads between each color change; no transition is necessary for the bugle beads. Place another piece of tape on the thread to keep the beads in place.

Step 2: Repeat Step 1 for a total of 13 strands.

Step 3: Cut the wire into two 5" (13 cm) pieces. Begin forming a wrapped loop about 1" (2.5 cm) from the end of each wire, but do not wrap the loops yet. Set aside.

Step 4: Remove the tape from one end of each strand. Gather the ends together and tie an overhand knot by using one jaw of the round-nose pliers to slide the knot as close to the beads as possible. Slip a wire loop into the knot as you remove the pliers, then pull the knot tight. Tie a square knot with the thread ends and dab the knot with glue. Let dry, then trim the threads close to the knot. Repeat for the other end of the strands, making sure there are no gaps between beads before you tie the knot.

Step 5: Complete the wrapped loops. String 1 cone and 1 size 8°. Pull the wrapped loop and knot up inside the cone. Form another wrapped loop including one half of the clasp. Repeat for the other side of the necklace.

MATERIALS

Size 11° seed beads in transparent dark blue, silver-lined dark blue, transparent medium blue, silver-lined medium blue, pearl-finish pale blue, and clear
3mm clear AB bugle beads
2 size 8° transparent dark blue seed beads
2 sterling silver 15mm cones
Sterling silver lobster clasp
Sterling silver soldered jump ring
G-S Hypo Cement
10" (25.4 cm) of 24-gauge sterling silver wire
27" (69 cm) of .006 braided beading thread

TOOLS

Size 10 beading needle
Scissors
Tape
Wire cutters
Chain-nose pliers
Round-nose pliers

FINISHED SIZE

17" (43 cm)

RESOURCES

All materials: Fusion Beads.

dsay Burke

Inspired by Japan's famous pearls, Lindsay creat this necklace using Swarovski pearls, which give richness to the piece without the huge price tag. T asymmetrical design of the piece gives the illusion the pearls "blowing" in from the east.

Step 1: Cut the end of an 18" (46 cm) piece of ribbon to a very shallow angle. String 1 crimp tube and 1 soldered jump ring. Pass back through the tube and crimp. Cover with a crimp cover. Trim the tail end of the ribbon. Cut the other end of the ribbon at a very shallow angle.

Step 2: String one 10mm pearl, two 12mm pearls, one 10mm pearl, one 10mm crystal, one 8mm pearl, two 6mm crystals, one 6mm pearl, and two 6mm crystals.

Step 3: String 1 crimp tube and the second soldered jump ring. Pass back through the tube; crimp and cover.

Step 4: Repeat Step 1. String one 12mm pearl, one 10mm crystal, two 10mm pearls, one 8mm crystal, one 6mm crystal, one 8mm pearl, one 6mm crystal, and one 6mm pearl. Repeat Step 3.

Step 5: Repeat Step 1. String one 12mm pearl, one 10mm pearl, one 10mm crystal, two 8mm pearls, one 8mm crystal, one 6mm crystal, and one 6mm pearl. Repeat

Step 6: Repeat Step 1. String two 12mm pearls, one 10 pearl, one 12mm pearl, one 10mm pearl, two 8 pearls, and one 6mm pearl. Repeat Step 3.

Step 7: Use the head pin to string one 12mm pearl. F a wrapped loop that attaches to one end of the cl Use two jump rings to attach the other end of the c to one soldered ring. Use two jump rings to attach lobster clasp to the other soldered ring.

Step 8: Spread the beads out on each strand of ribbon, ing 1" (2.5 cm) between large beads and up to 3" (7.6 between small beads.

RESOURCES

Bubbles

The Thiens and Karen Villagers

There is a baby in the Karen Village in
Thailand who brings joy to all who meet
her. This necklace is inspired by her ability
to laugh at nearly anything. The rope rings
were made by her mother especially for
this piece.

MATERIALS

4 white 8–12mm coin pearls
7 lace agate 12mm rounds
3 Thai silver 8mm rounds
2 Thai silver 12mm coins
2 Thai silver 18mm coins
40 Thai silver 8mm jump rings
19 Thai silver 12mm rope rings
Thai silver S-clasp
8" (20 cm) of 24-gauge sterling silver wire
25" (63.5 cm) of 22-gauge sterling silver wire

TOOLS

Wire cutters
Round-nose pliers
Flat-nose pliers

FINISHED SIZE

18" (46 cm)

Step 1: Use 2" (5 cm) of 24-gauge wire to form a double
simple loop. String 1 pearl and form a double simple
loop. Repeat three times for a total of four links.

Step 2: Use 1" (2.5 cm) of 22-gauge wire to form a simple
loop. String 1 silver round and form a simple loop.
Repeat twice for a total of three links.

Step 3: Use 2" (5 cm) of 22-gauge wire to form a simple loop.
String 1 coin and form a wrapped loop. Repeat for each
coin and the agate rounds for a total of eleven links.

Step 4: Connect rope rings and links as follows, using 1 jump
ring between each: 1 rope ring, 1 lace agate link, 5 rope
rings, 1 rope ring and 1 jump ring together, 1 rope ring,
1 lace agate link, 1 rope ring, 1 pearl link, 1 rope ring, one

link, 1 rope ring, 1 pearl link, 1 rope ring, 1 lace agate link,
one 12mm coin link, 1 rope ring, 1 rope ring and jump
ring together, and the clasp.

Step 5: Use 1 jump ring to attach 1 silver link to the ninth
rope ring. Connect as before, starting with the silver link:
1 lace agate link, 1 rope ring, 1 pearl link, one 18mm
coin link, 1 lace agate link, 1 rope ring, 1 lace agate link,
1 silver link, and the fifteenth rope link.

RESOURCES

All materials: Shiana.

TIP

For a variety of colors, use other stone and pearl beads. The
clasp can hook to any ring of the necklace for a variety of

Zephyr

Danielle Fox

This multistrand necklace features a melodious mixture of transparent and matte clear beads. The six strands are twisted together and finished with textured silver cones.

MATERIALS

156 clear size 11° seed beads
342 white-lined clear size 11° seed beads
57 clear 6mm glass coins
50 clear 7mm fire-polished rounds
32 clear opaque 11×9mm flat glass ovals
26 clear 14×8mm glass ovals
16 clear 25×12mm twisted glass ovals
2 sterling silver 10×22mm cones
2 silver 3×3mm crimp tubes
14 silver 2mm crimp tubes
2 sterling silver crimp covers
120" (305 cm) of .019 beading wire

TOOLS

Wire cutters
Crimping pliers
Mighty crimping pliers

FINISHED SIZE

19½" (49.5 cm)

Step 1: Cut the wire into six 20" (51 cm) pieces. String a crimp tube on one end of each wire and crimp 1½" from the end; do not trim the wires.

Step 2: Use one wire to string 1 clear size 11° seed bead and 1 white-lined size 11° seed bead 156 times. String a 2mm crimp tube and crimp, making sure that the beads are snug but not tight. Do not trim the wire.

Step 3: Repeat Step 2, stringing 1 white-lined size 11° and 1 coin fifty-seven times; string 1 white-lined clear size 11°.

Step 4: Repeat Step 2, stringing 1 white-lined size 11° and 1 clear round fifty times; string 1 white-lined size 11°.

Step 5: Repeat Step 2, stringing 1 white-lined size 11° and 1 flat oval thirty-two times; string 1 white-lined size 11°.

Step 6: Repeat Step 2, stringing 1 white-lined size 11° and 1 glass oval twenty-six times; string 1 white-lined size 11°.

Step 7: Repeat Step 2, stringing 1 white-lined size 11° and 1 twisted oval sixteen times; string 1 white-lined size 11°.

Step 8: Hold all six wires together to string a 3mm crimp tube; crimp. Trim all but two wires and use them to string a cone, a 2mm crimp tube, and one half of the clasp; pass back through the tube and crimp. Trim excess wire and cover the crimp with a crimp cover.

Step 9: Repeat Step 8 for the other half of the necklace, twisting the strands slightly before crimping.

RESOURCES

Clear glass beads: Bokamo Designs. Cones and clasp: Springall Adventures. Crimp covers: Fusion Beads.

Waterfall

Jamie Hogsett

Fluid and flowing like a waterfall at dusk, this three-strand necklace expresses glitz and glamour like no other.

MATERIALS
42 light azore satin 4mm Swarovski crystal rounds
58 peacock gray 7mm freshwater pearls
36 Indian sapphire 8mm Swarovski crystal rounds
15 green/gray/teal 12mm mother-of-pearl rounds
166 Thai silver 3mm cones
Three-strand sterling silver hook-and-eye clasp
6 sterling silver 2mm crimp tubes
63" (160 cm) of .014 beading wire

TOOLS
Wire cutters
Crimping pliers

FINISHED SIZE
16½" (42 cm) (shortest strand)

TIP
Alternate the stringing direction of each cone to add visual movement to the necklace. For two cones, string them with the wide ends touching.

Step 1: Attach 19" (48 cm) of wire to the first hole of one half of the clasp using a crimp tube.

Step 2: String 1 cone, one 4mm round, 1 cone, and one 8mm round three times. String 1 cone and one 4mm round. String 1 cone and 1 pearl nine times. String 1 cone, one 4mm round, 1 cone, and one 8mm round three times. String 1 cone, one 12mm round, and 2 cones.

Step 3: String one 12mm round and repeat Step 2, reversing the stringing sequence. String 1 crimp tube and the first hole of the other half of the clasp. Pass back through the tube and crimp.

Step 4: Attach 21" (53 cm) of wire to the middle hole of one half of the clasp using a crimp tube. Repeat Step 2. String one 12mm round and 2 cones twice. String one 12mm round and repeat Step 2, reversing the order. String 1 crimp tube and the middle hole of the other half of the clasp. Pass back through the tube and crimp.

Step 5: Attach 23" (58 cm) of wire to the last hole of one half of the clasp using a crimp tube. String 1 cone, one 4mm round, 1 cone, and one 8mm round three times. String 1 cone and one 4mm round. String 1 cone and 1 pearl eleven times. String 1 cone, one 4mm round, 1 cone, and one 8mm round three times. String 1 cone. String one 12mm round and 2 cones three times. String one 12mm round and repeat, reversing the stringing sequence and attaching the other half of the clasp.

RESOURCES
Crystals and clasp: Fusion Beads. Mother-of-pearl beads: Soft Flex Company. Thai silver: The Bead Goes On.

Storm Winds

Cynthia Thornton

A ncient civilizations, the dusky color of clouds before a thunderstorm, and the peace that follows a heavy rain are the inspirations for this necklace.

MATERIALS
- 61 labradorite 4mm faceted rondelles
- 2 dark kyanite 10×14mm ovals
- 2 pale kyanite 13×18mm ovals
- 2 dark kyanite 12×14mm faceted ovals
- 10 sterling silver 3mm cornerless cubes
- 1 sterling silver 3×8mm tube
- 8 sterling silver 4mm spacers
- 12 sterling silver 8mm spacers
- 12 sterling silver 20mm paddles
- 2 pewter 15mm pendants
- 1 pewter 25mm pendant
- 3 sterling silver 2mm crimp tubes
- Pewter hook-and-eye clasp
- 4" (10 cm) of 22-gauge sterling silver wire
- 40" (102 cm) of silk cord
- 14" (36 cm) of .014 beading wire

TOOLS
Wire cutters
Crimping pliers
Chain-nose pliers

FINISHED SIZE
18" (46 cm)

Step 1: Use 2" (5 cm) of beading wire to string 1 cornerless cube and 1 labradorite nine times. String 1 cornerless cube, the 25mm pendant, and 1 crimp tube. Pass the other end of the beading wire through the tube to form a circle and crimp the tube.

Step 2: Use 12" (30.5 cm) of beading wire to *string 1 crimp tube and 26 labradorite. Pass back through the tube to form a loop at the end of the wire, then crimp the tube.

Step 3: String one 8mm spacer, one 10×14mm oval, one 8mm spacer, 1 paddle, one 4mm spacer, 1 paddle, one 4mm spacer, 1 paddle, one 8mm spacer, one 13×18mm oval, one 8mm spacer, 1 paddle, one 4mm spacer, 1 paddle, one 4mm spacer, 1 paddle, one 8mm spacer, 1 faceted oval, and one 8mm spacer.

Step 4: String the tube and the circle formed in Step 1, then repeat Step 3, reversing the sequence. Repeat Step 2 from *.

Step 5: String one of the labradorite loops to the center of two 10" (25 cm) pieces of silk cord. Use all four ends of cord to string one 15mm pendant and one half of the clasp. Position the pendant ½" (1 cm) from the labradorite loop and the clasp ½" (1 cm)rom the end of the cord. Fold the cord ends back toward the pendant and use 2" (5 cm) of sterling wire to wrap the cords together. Repeat entire step for the other half of the necklace.

RESOURCES
Pewter pendants and clasp: Green Girl Studios.
Labradorite and kyanite: Chevron Trading Post & Bead Company. Sterling silver paddles and spacers: Kamol (wholesale only).

TIP
Use a folded piece of 22-gauge wire to help pass the ends of silk through the pendant and clasp openings.

Sweet Dream

Jaida Kimmerer

Cubic zirconia and crystal rounds, coupled with multiple strands of silver cubes, make this piece gorgeous, sparkly, and sophisticated. Jaida created it to evoke a feeling of being on Cloud Nine.

MATERIALS

51 white cubic zirconia 4mm faceted rondelles
60 light azore 4mm Swarovski crystal rounds
1 blue 45mm etched shell pendant
510 Thai silver 3mm squares
2 sterling silver 6×22mm cones
Sterling silver moon-and-star-toggle clasp
8 sterling silver 2mm crimp tubes
1 sterling silver 7mm jump ring
2 sterling silver 22-gauge eye pins
6' (183 cm) of .014 beading wire

TOOLS

Crimping pliers
Wire cutters
Chain-nose pliers
Round-nose pliers

FINISHED SIZE

16¾" (43 cm)

Step 1: Attach 18" (46 cm) of wire to one eye pin using a crimp tube. String 170 squares, 1 crimp tube, and the other eye pin. Pass back through the tube and crimp. Repeat entire step twice more.

Step 2: Open the jump ring and attach it to the pendant. Close the jump ring around the center of all three strands made in Step 1.

Step 3: Attach 18" (46 cm) of wire to one eye pin using a crimp tube. String 2 rounds and 1 rondelle fifteen times. String 21 rondelles. String 1 rondelle and 2 rounds fifteen times. String 1 crimp tube and the other eye pin. Pass back through the tube and crimp.

Step 4: Use an eye pin to string 1 cone. Form a wrapped loop that attaches to one half of the clasp. Repeat entire step for the other half of the necklace.

RESOURCES

Pendant: Lillypilly Designs, Inc. All other materials: Fusion Beads.

Icy Elegance

Elizabeth Chumtong

Beautiful rainbow moonstone beads are the inspiration for this piece. Use the necklace to accent a little black dress for a holiday party or a silk shirt with a plunging neckline for a night at the ballet.

MATERIALS

30 rainbow 8×10mm moonstone rectangles
106 Thai silver 2mm cornerless cubes
6 round 3mm silver beads
Sterling silver two-to-one spacer
Sterling silver toggle clasp
2 sterling silver 2" (5 cm) head pins
5 sterling silver 2mm crimp tubes
30" (76 cm) of .019 beading wire

TOOLS

Wire cutters
Crimping pliers
Round-nose pliers

FINISHED SIZE

16" (41 cm)

Step 1: Attach 24" (61 cm) of wire to one half of the clasp using a crimp tube. String one 3mm and 3 cubes. String one moonstone and 2 cubes fourteen times.

Step 2: Pass down through the two-hole side of the spacer, then up through the same side. Repeat Step 1, reversing the sequence.

Step 3: String two moonstone and one 3mm on a head pin and form a wrapped loop. Repeat once. Set aside.

Step 4: Pass 6" (15 cm) of wire through the bottom loop on the back of the spacer. Fold the wire in half, hold the ends together, string a crimp tube up to the spacer, and crimp.

Step 5: On one end of the wire string 20 cubes, one 3mm, 1 crimp tube, and one of the dangles made in Step 3. Pass back through the tube and crimp.

Step 6: Repeat Step 5 with the other end of the wire, stringing 24 cubes this time.

RESOURCES

All materials: Saki Silver.

Stone Cold

Mike Sherman

Cool weather can't compare to the cool design of this frosty necklace. Labradorite and onyx beads trickle down the sides to meet a large quartz teardrop that's a real hunk of ice.

Step 1: Attach the wire to one half of the clasp using a crimp tube.

Step 2: String 10 rondelles. String 1 nugget and 1 rondelle three times. String 1 briolette and 1 rondelle. String 1 nugget, 1 rondelle, 1 briolette, and 1 rondelle twice. String 3 spiral-cut teardrops, one 20mm teardrop, 3 spiral-cut teardrops, 1 rondelle, 1 briolette, 1 rondelle, 1 nugget, 1 rondelle, 1 briolette, 1 rondelle, and 3 spiral-cut teardrops.

Step 3: String the 30mm teardrop. Repeat Step 2, reversing the stringing sequence.

Step 4: String 1 crimp tube and the other side of the clasp. Pass back through the tube and crimp.

RESOURCES

All materials: Soft Flex Company.

MATERIALS

44 black tourmaline 6mm rondelles

10 black onyx 14mm briolettes

18 spiral-cut 8×12mm quartz crystal teardrops

12 labradorite 18mm nuggets

2 rutilated quartz 20mm teardrops

30mm rutilated quartz teardrop

2 sterling silver 3mm crimp tubes

Sterling silver toggle clasp

24" (61 cm) of .024 beading wire

TOOLS

Wire cutters

Crimping pliers

FINISHED SIZE

18" (46 cm)

Aquatic Petroglyphs

Dustin Wedekind

Colors and shapes harmonize in this piece like a message to the fish from a sandy shore. The pyrite in the New Mexico turquoise picks up the textures of the lampworked glass beads.

MATERIALS

28 New Mexico turquoise 5×10mm rectangles
5 agate 15mm diamonds
4 lampworked 18mm glass squares
37 pyrite 4mm spacers
4 Thai silver 8mm spacers
Sterling silver toggle clasp
2 sterling silver 2mm crimp tubes
26" (66 cm) of .019 beading wire

TOOLS

Wire cutters
Crimping pliers

FINISHED SIZE

18½" (47 cm)

Step 1: String 1 pyrite to the center of the wire. Use both ends to string 1 silver spacer, 1 lampworked, 1 silver spacer, 1 agate, 1 silver spacer, 1 lampworked, and 1 silver spacer.

Step 2: Use one end of the wire to string 1 pyrite, 1 rectangle, 1 pyrite, 1 agate, 1 pyrite, 1 rectangle, 1 pyrite, 1 lampworked, 1 pyrite, 1 rectangle, 1 pyrite, 1 agate, and 1 pyrite. String 1 rectangle and 1 pyrite eleven times. String 1 crimp tube and one half of the clasp. Pass back through the tube and crimp.

Step 3: Repeat Step 2 with the other end of the wire and the other half of the clasp.

RESOURCES

Turquoise rectangles and pyrite spacers: New Mexico Bead Trader. Agate: Thunderbird Supply Company. Silver spacers: The Bead Goes On. Clasp: Saki Silver. Lampworked beads: Desert Bloom Designs.

Skipping Stones

Jamie Hogsett

Handmade tabular beads in varying shades of blue resemble the way that water ripples when stones bounce across it, with crystals dangling like sparkling droplets.

Step 1: Use a head pin to string 1 bicone; form a wrapped loop that attaches to a soldered ring. Repeat to attach one of each color of bicone to each soldered ring (three per ring). You will have 22 Pacific opal bicones left over to complete the necklace.

Step 2: Use 4" (10 cm) of wire to form a wrapped loop that attaches to one half of the clasp. String 1 bicone, 1 rondelle, and 1 bicone. Form a wrapped loop that attaches to one of the soldered rings.

Step 3: Use 5" (13 cm) of wire to form a wrapped loop that attaches to the previous ring. String 1 bicone, 1 porcelain, and 1 bicone. Form a wrapped loop that attaches to another ring. Repeat entire step eight times.

Step 4: Use 4" (10 cm) of wire to form a wrapped loop that attaches to the last ring. String 1 bicone, 1 rondelle, and 1 bicone. Form a wrapped loop that attaches to the other half of the clasp. Before making the final wrap, check to make sure there are no twists in the components so that the necklace will lie flat.

RESOURCES

Porcelain beads: Some Enchanted Beading. Crystals: Beyond Beadery and Fusion Beads. Clasp: Star's Clasps.

NOTE

For thicker wrapped loops, like the ones shown here, wrap the wire back toward the loop before trimming.

MATERIALS

10 silk 4mm Swarovski crystal bicones
10 khaki 4mm Swarovski crystal bicones
32 Pacific opal 4mm Swarovski crystal bicones
2 silk 6×8mm Swarovski crystal rondelles
9 tabular 20×24mm porcelain beads
10 sterling silver 6mm soldered jump rings
Sterling silver box clasp with stone inlay
30 sterling silver 22-gauge 2" (5 cm) head pins
53" (135 cm) of 22-gauge sterling silver wire

TOOLS

Wire cutters
Flat-nose pliers
Round-nose pliers
Crimping pliers

FINISHED SIZE

17" (43 cm)

Picture Window

Suzy Cox

Alineup of agate cut-outs is what gives this bracelet its sassy 1960s-style flavor. Make sure to show this one off by wearing it with short sleeves only!

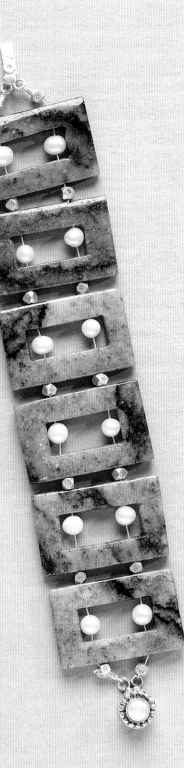

MATERIALS

12 white oval 6mm freshwater pearls
6 blue agate 25×40mm double-drilled open, flat rectangles
14 Hill tribe silver 4mm faceted cubes with flower design
4 sterling silver 2mm crimp tubes
Double-strand sterling silver clasp with pearl inlay
20" (50 cm) of .019 sterling silver nylon-coated beading wire

TOOLS

Wire cutters
Crimping pliers

FINISHED SIZE

8" (20 cm)

Step 1: Attach 10" (25 cm) of beading wire to the right-hand loop on one half of the clasp using a crimp tube. String 1 cube.

Step 2: Pass through the right-hand hole of 1 rectangle, pulling the wire up through the middle of the rectangle. String 1 pearl and pass through the right-hand hole on the other half of the rectangle. String 1 cube.

Step 3: Repeat Step 2 with the remaining rectangles.

Step 4: String 1 crimp tube and the opposite loop on the second half of the clasp. Pass back through the crimp tube and crimp.

Step 5: Repeat Steps 1 through 4, working the left-hand side of the bracelet.

RESOURCES

Stones: Dakota Enterprises.
Clasp: Star's Clasps.

ChChChains

Anna Karena

Much like the experience of listening to Aretha's famous song, this jumble of chains and stones visually dances with its vibrant and random patterning.

MATERIALS

- 2 chalcedony 6×10mm faceted ovals
- 1 kyanite 7×14mm flat oval
- 2 chalcedony 10mm coins
- 2 akynite 10mm coins
- 3 synthetic quartz 8×12 faceted rectangles
- 3 London blue topaz 8×12mm faceted flat teardrops
- 2 chalcedony 9×11mm flat triangles
- 1 chalcedony 12mm square pillow
- 2 prehnite 12×17mm rough-cut tear drops
- 11" (27.5 cm) of sterling silver 6×8mm smooth, flat oval chain
- 9" (22.5 cm) of sterling silver 7×10mm hammered oval chain
- 10" (25 cm) of sterling silver 4×20mm hammered oval chain
- 13" (32.5 cm) of sterling silver 8mm twisted oval and circle chain
- 6 sterling silver 6mm jump rings
- Sterling silver hook-and-eye clasp with patterned links
- 54" (135 cm) of 24-gauge half-hard sterling silver wire

TOOLS

- Wire cutters
- Chain-nose pliers
- Round-nose pliers

FINISHED SIZE

18" (45 cm) (length of shortest strand)

Step 1: Open 1 jump ring and string one half of the clasp and the end of the 6×8mm chain. Close the jump ring. Cut the sixth link of chain.

Step 2: Cut a 4" (10 cm) length of wire and form a wrapped loop that attaches to the end link of the chain from Step 1. String 1 kyanite and form a wrapped loop that attaches to the end link of the remaining 6×8mm chain.

Step 3: Continue down the chain, randomly adding stone links and lengths of chain as in Step 2. Once you reach the desired length, add a jump ring and the other half of the clasp.

Step 4: Cut an 11-link length of the 7×10mm chain and place an open jump ring on each end link.

Step 5: Lay the strand made in Steps 1–3 on the work surface. Set the 11-link 7×10mm chain section next to the long strand so it lies parallel, across the middle. Attach the jump rings to the closest links on the long strand so the 7×10mm chain is attached.

Step 6: Repeat Steps 1–3, this time using the 8mm chain with short lengths of the 7×10mm chain interspersed. Stagger your stone segments so they don't lie next to the stone segments placed on the first strand. Use all the chain so this strand is longer than the first.

Step 7: Repeat Step 6 using the 4×20mm chain with short lengths of the 7×10mm chain interspersed.

RESOURCES

All materials: The Bead Monkey.

Ice Storm

Kate McKinnon

Filled with glittering rhinestones, pearls, and silver, this bracelet reminds Kate of seed heads and winter foliage covered with a sparkling layer of ice.

Step 1: String 1 pearl on a head pin and form a wrapped loop. Repeat to make 72 dangles with all the pearls.

Step 2: Form a wrapped loop at one end of the sterling wire. Form another loop that attaches to the bar side of the clasp. String 1 crimp tube to the center of a 4" (10 cm) piece of beading wire. On one end, string 1 triangle and the open wrapped loop. Pass back through the triangle and tube. On the other end of the wire, string 1 triangle and the soldered jump ring. Pass back through the triangle and the tube, then crimp.

Step 3: String 1 crimp tube, 1 triangle, and the soldered jump ring on the end of a 10" (25 cm) piece of wire. Pass back through the triangle and the tube, then crimp.

Step 4: String 2 triangles, 3 Delicas, 3 dangles, 1 button, 3 Delicas, and 3 dangles five times, alternating buttons and leaves. You will end with a leaf. (The dangles will slide back and forth over the Delicas.) String 1 triangle, 1 crimp tube, and the ring side of the clasp. Pass back through the tube and crimp.

Step 5: Repeat Step 3.

Step 6: Repeat Step 4, beginning with a leaf and ending with a button.

RESOURCES

Delicas: Caravan Beads; glass leaves: Eclectica; rhinestone buttons: fabric or notions stores; soldered rings and sterling wire: Rio Grande; clasp: Kate McKinnon.

MATERIALS

68 rhodium-plated Delicas
72 silver 3mm freshwater pearls
6 clear 8mm Czech glass leaves
29 Thai silver 6mm triangles
6 silver 8mm shank buttons with clear rhinestone inlays
12mm soldered sterling silver jump ring
3"(8 cm) of 19-gauge sterling wire
72 silver 2" (5 cm) head pins
Fine silver toggle clasp
5 sterling silver 2mm crimp tubes
24" (61 cm) of .019 beading wire

TOOLS

Round-nose pliers
Flat-nose pliers
Crimping pliers
Wire cutters

FINISHED SIZE

7" (18 cm)

TIP

For strength, double wrap the pearls by wrapping down to the base of each pearl, then back up to the loop. Doing so not only prevents you from nicking the soft surface of the pearls with the cutters, but allows you to trim the wire at the loop for a clean cut.

Khumbu Icefall

Heather Culhane

Khumbu Icefall, an eerie place on the Everest glacier where climbers often tumble, is the inspiration for this icicle-encrusted necklace. Heather has tried to re-create the spooky feeling of Khumbu by designing a piece that compels people to touch it, yet draws them back at the last minute.

MATERIALS

8 clear 6mm AB Swarovski crystal bicones
6 faceted 14mm aquamarine briolettes
12 spiked 20–25mm kyanite crystals
4 lampworked 13mm lentils
2 lampworked 15mm porcupine beads
2 lampworked 18mm porcupine beads
30mm lampworked porcupine focal bead
6 lampworked 60mm spiral etched icicles
2 Italian silver 50mm custom-made talons
8 Thai silver 60mm icicles
12 Thai silver 5mm bicones
16 Thai silver 5mm coils
6 Thai silver 7mm carved beads
Sterling silver toggle clasp
4 sterling silver 2mm crimp tubes
20" (51 cm) of .019 beading wire

TOOLS

Wire cutters
Crimping pliers

FINISHED SIZE

16" (41 cm)

Step 1: Attach the wire to one half of the clasp using a crimp tube.

Step 2: String 3 silver bicones, 1 briolette, 1 silver bicone, 1 briolette, 1 coil, 1 lentil, 1 coil, 1 briolette, 1 coil, 1 lentil, 1 coil, 2 kyanite, 1 coil, one 15mm porcupine, 1 coil, 1 silver icicle, 1 crystal, 2 kyanite, 1 silver bicone, 1 glass icicle, 1 silver bicone, 2 kyanite, 1 crystal, 1 silver icicle, 1 carved bead, one 18mm porcupine, 1 carved bead, 1 glass icicle, 1 crystal, 1 silver icicle, 1 coil, 1 talon, 1 coil, 1 silver icicle, 1 crystal, 1 glass icicle, and 1 carved bead.

Step 3: String the 30mm porcupine focal bead. Repeat Step 2, reversing the sequence. String 1 crimp tube and the other half of the clasp. Pass back through the tube and crimp.

RESOURCES

Lampworked glass lentils and porcupine beads: Linda Podkova of Moonbeads; etched icicles: Wes Sanders of Immortal Dragon Art; Thai silver: Shiana.

Under the Sea

Tamara L. Honaman

Design inspiration can come from anywhere, and in this case it came from a handful of fanciful lampworked beads. Once the seed, cube, and silver beads were added, this piece just flowed with creativity.

MATERIALS

4–7 lampworked beads
Assortment of seed, triangle, and cube beads to complement lampworked beads
8 silver 5×7mm top-drilled freshwater pearls
6 sterling silver 5mm rounds
8 sterling silver 6mm rounds
2 sterling silver 8mm rounds
2 Bali silver 8mm granulated rounds
2 Bali silver 12mm granulated saucers
1 Thai silver 18mm shell
1 sterling silver 26mm hammered round
Handmade fine silver toggle clasp
2 sterling silver 2mm crimp tubes
60" (150 cm) of .019 beading wire

TOOLS

Chain-nose pliers
Wire cutters

FINISHED SIZE

23" (58.4 cm)

RESOURCES

Toggle: Tamara Honaman.
Lampworked nautilus: Wildfire Designs.
Lampworked tubes: Nancy Tobey.
Lampworked rondelles: Family Glass.
Wire and crimps: Fire Mountain Gems.

Step 1: Cut two 30" (75 cm) pieces of beading wire. Pair the wire ends and string 1 crimp tube, 1 cube, and the bar half of the clasp. Pass back through the cube and crimp tube and crimp.

Step 2: Keeping the wires paired, string ½" (1.3 cm) of assorted cube, seed, and triangle beads and 5mm round. Separate the wire ends. String assorted seed, triangle, and cube beads onto each wire for about 1" (2.5 cm). Pair the wire ends and string one 5mm round. Separate the wires again and string 1" (2.5 cm) of assorted beads on each wire.

Step 3: Pair the wire ends and string 1 Bali 8mm round. Separate the wires and string 3½" (8.85 cm) of assorted cube and seed beads on one wire and 4" (10 cm) on the other. (The difference in lengths will cause one wire to curve outward and separate the wires.

Step 4: Pair the wire ends and string the silver shell. Separate the wires and string 1½" (4 cm) of assorted seed, triangle, cube, pearl, seamless round, and tube beads on one wire and 2½" (10 cm) on the other. Repeat three more times, the first time using a rondelle when you pair the wire ends, the second time the hammered round, and the third time a rondelle.

Step 5: Pair the wire ends and string 1 seamless 8mm round, the nautilus, and 1 seamless 8mm round. Separate the wires and string 3½" (9 cm) of assorted beads on one wire and 4" (10 cm) on the other.

Step 6: Pair the wire ends and string 1 Bali 8mm round. Separate the wires and string 1" (2.5 cm) of assorted cube and seed beads on each wire. Pair the wire ends and string one 5mm round. Separate the wires and string 1" (2.5 cm) of assorted cube and seed beads on each wire.

Step 7: Pair the wire ends and string one 5mm round, ½" (1.3 cm) of assorted beads, 1 crimp tube, and 1 cube.

Step 8: Separate the wires. String about 16 seed beads onto one wire and pass through the opening of the toggle and back through the cube and crimp tube. Repeat for the other wire. Snug the beads, but leave a little slack in the wires so the necklace drapes nicely; crimp.

Midnight Sea

Marlene Blessing

Based on its texture alone, this dramatic silver toggle clasp looks like it might have rested on the ocean's floor until found by some lucky diver. The kelplike color of the jade and the blue-black of the pearls add to the watery feel of this necklace, while the mottled lampworked beads mirror the toggle's rough beauty.

MATERIALS
27 light blue size 8° seed beads
120 peacock blue 6mm freshwater pearls
48 jade 8mm faceted rondelles
10 lampworked 12mm glass beads
Sterling silver toggle clasp
4 sterling silver Twisted Tornado crimp tubes
50" (127 cm) of .019 beading wire

TOOLS
Wire cutters
Flat-nose pliers

FINISHED SIZE
21½" (55 cm) (shortest strand)

Step 1: Attach 25" (63.5 cm) of wire to one half of the clasp using a crimp tube. String 3 seed beads, 6 pearls, 1 rondelle, 1 seed bead, 1 pearl, 1 seed bead, 9 rondelles, 1 seed bead, 1 pearl, 1 seed bead, 8 rondelles, 1 seed bead, 1 pearl, 1 seed bead, 8 pearls, 1 seed bead, 8 pearls, 1 seed bead, 8 pearls, 1 seed bead, 8 pearls, 1 seed bead, 1 pearl, 1 seed bead, 8 rondelles, 1 seed bead, 1 pearl, 1 seed bead, 9 rondelles, 1 seed bead, 1 pearl, 1 seed bead, 1 rondelle, 6 pearls, 3 seed beads, 1 crimp tube, and the other half of the clasp. Pass back through the tube and crimp.

Step 2: Attach 25" (63.5 cm) of wire to one half of the clasp using a crimp tube. String 3 seed beads, 4 pearls, 1 rondelle, 1 pearl, and 1 lampworked bead. String 1 pearl, 1 rondelle, 1 pearl, and 1 lampworked bead four times. String 8 pearls, 1 rondelle, 28 pearls, 1 rondelle, and 8 pearls. String 1 lampworked bead, 1 pearl, 1 rondelle, and 1 pearl five times. String 3 pearls, 3 seed beads, 1 crimp tube, and the other half of the clasp. Pass back through the tube and crimp.

RESOURCES

Seed beads: Knot Just Beads. Jade and pearls: Lucky Gems & Jewelry (wholesale only). Lampworked glass beads: Mother Beads. Clasp: Saki Silver.

Tourmaline Tango

Laura Levaas

Multicolored tourmaline is interesting to work with—no two beads are exactly alike, and each individual nugget or chip can reveal an array of colors. Detailed pewter donuts create an attractive centerpiece, which can be removed for a lighter dance step.

MATERIALS

320 tourmaline 5mm cubes
4 pewter 20–25mm rings
Sterling silver toggle clasp
8 sterling silver 2mm crimp tubes
72" (183 cm) of .014 beading wire

TOOLS

Wire cutters
Crimping pliers

FINISHED SIZE

16½" (42 cm)

Step 1: Attach 18" (46 cm) of wire to one half of the clasp using a crimp tube. String 80 cubes, grouping them roughly by color, 1 crimp tube, and the other half of the clasp. Pass back through the tube and crimp.

Step 2: Repeat Step 1 three times.

Step 3: Slide the donuts over the toggle bar so they hang in the middle of the necklace.

RESOURCES

Clasp: Kipuka Trading. Donuts: Green Girl Studios. Tourmaline: Fire Mountain Gems and Beads.

Twofer

Tamara L. Honaman

This piece offers a two-for-one deal. Wear it as two bracelets and you've got a trendy combo; connect the bracelets' ends, and you've got an outrageously cool necklace!

MATERIALS

Mix of gemstone beads and pearls 3–8mm

6 sterling silver 3mm rounds

6 Thai silver tube beads with opening (optional)

64–100 sterling silver 7.33mm jump rings

2 sterling silver 1-to-3 hole links

2 sterling silver 10mm lobster clasps

6 sterling silver 2mm crimp beads

30" (75 cm) of .014 beading wire

TOOLS

Flexible tape measure

2 flat-nose pliers

Wire cutters

Crimping pliers

FINISHED SIZE

8" (20 cm) as a bracelet, 16" (40 cm) as a necklace

3-Strand Bracelet

Step 1: Measure your wrist to determine your bracelet's length.

Step 2: Measure the length of the 2 links and 1 lobster clasp. Subtract this measurement from the desired finished length to determine the length of beads needed to add to the bracelet.

Step 3: Use 10" (25 cm) of beading wire to string 1 crimp bead, 1 sterling silver round, and one loop on one of the links. Pass back through the sterling silver round and the crimp bead; crimp. Repeat to add 1 wire to each hole of the link.

Step 4: String beads in a random or ordered pattern until you reach the length determined in Step 2. String 1 crimp bead, 1 sterling silver round, and one loop on the other link, making sure to pass through the opposite loop you used on the first link. Pass back through the sterling silver round and the crimp bead; crimp.

Step 5: Repeat Step 4 for the remaining wires.

Step 6: Attach 1 jump ring to the single loop on one end of the bracelet. Repeat for the other end. Add 1 clasp to the end of the bracelet.

Step 7: If desired, cover the crimp beads. Use the flat-nose pliers to carefully open one Thai silver tube. Slip the opening over one crimped crimp bead and carefully close the tube. Repeat until you've covered all six crimp beads. Set the bracelet aside.

Chain Bracelet

Step 8: Open all but 2 of the remaining jump rings. String the 2 closed jump rings onto 1 open jump ring; close the jump ring. Add another open jump ring through the same original two; close the jump ring. Separate the four jump rings so you have two sets of two. This is the start of your simple 2×2 chain.

Step 9: Add 1 jump ring to either set of two jump rings; close. Repeat, adding a second jump ring to the same place. Repeat, adding 2 jump rings to the 2 jump rings on the end, until you've reached the desired length minus the length of the clasp.

Step 10: Add 1 jump ring to each end of the chain. Add 1 clasp to the end of the chain.

RESOURCES

Chain and findings: Fire Mountain Gems.

Abacus

Jamie Hogsett

This laddered pattern of luscious lamp-worked and sparkling crystal beads adds up to just one thing: beauty! You'll garner numerous compliments when you wear it, and you'll also become a wrapped-loop pro when you make it.

MATERIALS

42 clear dark mocha-lined size 11° seed beads (A)

231 teal matte silver-lined size 11° seed beads (B)

178 gold green size 11° seed beads (C)

14 khaki 4mm Swarovski crystal bicones

7 khaki 8mm Swarovski crystal rounds

12 gold green with teal stripe 6×10mm lampworked rondelles

40mm fine silver 2-strand toggle clasp

7 sterling silver 2mm crimp tubes

59" (147.5 cm) of sterling silver 22-gauge wire

36" (90 cm) of .015 beading wire

TOOLS

Wire cutters

Nylon-jaw pliers

Flat-nose pliers

Round-nose pliers

Chain-nose pliers

Crimping pliers

Bead Stoppers

FINISHED SIZE

7½" (18.8 cm)

Step 1: Cut the 22-gauge wire into eighteen 3" (7.5 cm) pieces and one 5" (12.5 cm) piece. Use a 3" (7.5 cm) piece of wire to form a double wrapped loop with a ⅛" (3mm) hole. String 1B, 1 lampworked rondelle, and 1B and form a double wrapped loop. Repeat 11 times for a total of 12 lampworked links. Repeat, using 1A, 1 crystal round, and 1A, for a total of 6 crystal links.

Step 2: Use the 5" (12.5 cm) piece of wire to form a double wrapped loop with a ¼" (6mm) hole loop. String 1A, 1 crystal round, and 1A, and form another double large wrapped loop that attaches to the bar half of the clasp.

Step 3: Use 9" (22.5 cm) of beading wire to string 1 crimp tube, 10B, and one hole of the ring half of the clasp.

Pass back through the first B strung and the crimp tube; crimp. String 4B. String one side of one crystal link, 7B, one side of one lampworked link, and 7B six times. String 2B and 1 crimp tube. Secure the end with a stopper and set aside.

Step 4: Repeat Step 3 for the other hole of the ring half of the clasp, this time stringing the other side of the crystal links and adding new lampworked links. Undo the stopper and pass through the crimp tube added in Step 3. Use both wires to string 7B and the crystal link made in Step 2. Pass back through the tube and crimp.

Step 5: Use 9" (22.5 cm) of beading wire to string 1 crimp tube, 5C, one hole of the ring half of the clasp, and 4C. Pass back through the first C strung and the crimp tube; crimp. *String 5C, 1A, 1 crystal bicone, 1A, and 5C. Pass through the first lampworked link strung in Step 3. Repeat from * five times. String 5C, 1A, 1 crystal bicone, 1A, 5C, 1 crimp tube, 10C, and the crystal link made in Step 2. Pass back through the first C strung after the crimp tube and the crimp tube; crimp.

Step 6: Repeat Step 5 from the other hole of the ring half of the clasp.

RESOURCES

Seed beads and crystals: Beyond Beadery.

Lampworked beads: Bokamo Designs.

Clasp: Kate McKinnon.

Beading wire: Beadalon.

Vine

Nancy Norden Walters

Organic and flowing, this lovely necklace wraps around your neck in a graceful, beautiful way, and is much easier to make than it looks.

MATERIALS
- 22 sage green 5×7mm freshwater pearls
- 24 green/brown 7×9mm freshwater pearls
- 11 total of olivine, khaki, and lime 8mm Swarovski crystal rounds
- 19 sterling silver 4mm flower heishis with loop
- 11 sterling silver 5mm flower bead caps
- 23 Thai silver 3×16mm curved tubes
- Sterling silver toggle clasp
- 2 sterling silver 2mm crimp tubes
- 57 sterling silver 24-gauge head pins
- 24" (61 cm) of .019 beading wire

TOOLS
- Wire cutters
- Crimping pliers
- Round-nose pliers
- Flat-nose pliers

FINISHED SIZE
16½" (43 cm)

Step 1: Use a head pin to string 1 pearl and form a wrapped loop. Repeat with each pearl. Use a head pin to string 1 crystal and 1 bead cap and form a wrapped loop. Repeat with each crystal and bead cap.

Step 2: Attach the wire to one half of the clasp using a crimp tube. String 1 curved tube and 2–4 pearls, crystals, and/or heishis twenty-two times. String 1 curved tube, 1 crimp tube, and the other half of the clasp. Pass back through the tube and crimp.

RESOURCES

Curved tubes: Somerset Silver (wholesale only). All other materials: Blue Frog Beads.

My Ántonia

Jamie Hogsett

MATERIALS

10 g each size 11° seed beads in kelly green, olive green, gold green, and gold
208 peridot 4mm faceted rondelles
31 gold vermeil 3mm rondelles
30×45mm polymer clay heart
2 Vermeil 10mm cubes
1 gold-filled 5mm jump ring
2 gold-filled 2mm crimp tubes
Vermeil toggle clasp
6" (25 cm) of 22-gauge gold-filled wire
250" (635 cm) of green PowerPro thread
24" (61 cm) of gold .014 beading wire

TOOLS

Wire cutters
Round-nose pliers
Flat-nose pliers
Crimping pliers
Size 10 beading needle
Scissors

FINISHED SIZE

18¼" (46 cm) (shortest strand)

Named for one of Jamie's favorite books, this necklace represents the beauty of the land in a way that only author Willa Cather could describe.

Step 1: Attach the jump ring to the polymer heart. Use 3" (8 cm) of 22-gauge wire to form a wrapped loop. Repeat. Tie the end of a piece of PowerPro (as long as you can work with) to one of the loops.

Step 2: String 19" (48 cm) of kelly green seed beads with a vermeil rondelle every 3–6". String the other wrapped loop, snug the beads, and tie a knot. Repeat for two more strands.

Step 3: Repeat Step 2 to work three strands of olive green seed beads, three strands of gold green seed beads, and two strands gold seed beads. Begin new thread as necessary at either wrapped loop.

Step 4: String 5½" (24 cm) of gold seed beads, 1 vermeil rondelle, 42 peridot rondelles, 1 vermeil rondelle, and 5½" (24 cm) of gold seed beads. Tie a knot around the wrapped loop, trim.

Step 5: Attach the beading wire to one of the wrapped loops using a crimp tube. String 82 peridot, the polymer heart, 82 peridot, 1 crimp tube, and the other wrapped loop. Pass back through the tube and crimp.

Step 6: Use one wrapped-loop wire to string 1 vermeil cube and 1 peridot. Snug all of the strands up to hide the knots and the crimp tube inside the cube. Form a wrapped loop that attaches to one half of the clasp. Repeat with the other wrapped-loop wire.

RESOURCES

Polymer heart: CF Originals.
Seed beads: Bead Cache.
Gold vermeil beads and toggle: The Bead Goes On.
Peridot: Fusion Beads.

Caspian Mermaid

Jean Campbell

W hen you wear this multistranded necklace, you may just fancy yourself a beautiful water nymph emerging from cold Caspian seawaters. Or not. Either way, you'll look like a goddess when you wear it.

MATERIALS

49 serpentine 10×6mm barrels
94 serpentine 5mm rondelles
42 horizontally drilled 8×12mm freshwater pearl teardrops
44 pink 6mm Swarovski crystal bicones
30×50mm pink quartz horizontally drilled teardrop pendant
12×20mm sterling silver box clasp with pearl inlay
6 sterling silver 2mm crimp tubes
62" (157.5 cm) of .019 beading wire

TOOLS

Wire cutters
Crimping pliers

FINISHED SIZE

15½" (39 cm) (shortest strand)

Step 1: Attach 18" (46 cm) of wire to one half of the clasp using a crimp tube. String 1 barrel, 2 rondelles, 1 barrel, 1 bicone, 1 rondelle, 1 barrel, 1 rondelle, and 1 bicone seven times. String 1 barrel, 2 rondelles, 1 barrel, and 1 crimp tube. Pass through the other half of the clasp, back through the tube, and crimp.

Step 2: Attach 20" (51 cm) of wire to one half of the clasp using a crimp tube. String 1 barrel, 2 rondelles, 1 barrel, 1 bicone, 1 rondelle, 1 barrel, 1 rondelle, and 1 bicone eight times. String 1 barrel, 2 rondelles, 1 barrel, and 1 crimp tube. Pass through the other half of the clasp, back through the tube, and crimp.

Step 3: Attach 24" (61 cm) of wire to one side of the clasp using a crimp tube. String 1 rondelle, 1 pearl, 1 rondelle, 1 pearl, 1 rondelle, 1 pearl, and 1 bicone. String 1 pearl, 1 rondelle, 1 pearl, 1 rondelle, 1 pearl, and 1 bicone six times. String the pendant. String 1 bicone, 1 pearl, 1 rondelle, 1 pearl, 1 rondelle, and 1 pearl six times. String 1 bicone, 1 pearl, 1 rondelle, 1 pearl, 1 rondelle, 1 pearl, 1 rondelle, and 1 crimp tube. Pass through the other half of the clasp, back through the tube, and crimp.

RESOURCES

Serpentine beads: Thunderbird Supply; pearls: Soft Flex Company; crystals: Beyond Beadery; pendant: Global Curiosity (wholesale only).

Sweetheart

Abbie Enyart

While playing with ideas for bridesmaids' jewelry for her upcoming wedding, Abbie made this lovely necklace. Pearls are always perfect for nuptials, and the black chain and wire make the piece both dramatic and romantic.

MATERIALS

50 freshwater 6mm rice pearls
4 faceted 8mm pink glass rondelles
12×15mm pink glass briolette
2 black 6mm spacers
2 black crimp beads
Sterling silver toggle clasp
15" (38 cm) of 3mm black cable chain
16" (41 cm) of .014 beading wire
20" (51 cm) of 24-gauge black wire

TOOLS

Wire cutters
Flat-nose pliers
Round-nose pliers
Crimping pliers

FINISHED SIZE

15½" (39 cm) (short strand)

Step 1: Using 10" (25 cm) of 24-gauge wire, make a bail with the briolette, string 1 rondelle, and form a wrapped loop that attaches to the middle link of the chain.

Step 2: Attach 5" (13 cm) of 24-gauge wire to one half of the clasp by forming a wrapped loop. String 1 rondelle and form another wrapped loop that attaches to end of the chain. Repeat for the other half of the clasp and chain.

Step 3: Attach the beading wire to the wrapped loop at one end of the chain using a crimp bead. String 25 pearls, 1 spacer, 1 rondelle, 1 spacer, 25 pearls, and 1 crimp bead. Pass through the wrapped loop on the other side of the clasp, back through the bead, and crimp.

RESOURCES
Clasp: Bokamo Designs; all other materials: Bead Cache.

Purple Reign

Suzy Cox

This substantial piece is an adornment fit for a member of royalty. Royalty that might ride a purple motorcycle, for instance.

MATERIALS

100 iridescent purple size 8° seed beads

46 peridot–4mm chips

50 amethyst–6mm chips

23 amethyst 6mm faceted rounds

40 amethyst 8mm rounds

10 fluorite 8mm rounds

20 olivine glass 9×12mm flat ovals

12 amethyst 14×18mm polished nuggets

1 amethyst 45mm donut

10 sterling silver 3mm seamless rounds

7 sterling silver crimp tubes

12mm sterling silver toggle clasp

76" (190 cm) of .019 beading wire

TOOLS

Wire cutters
Crimping pliers

FINISHED SIZE

18" (45 cm) (shortest strand)

Step 1: Cut two 26" (65 cm) pieces of beading wire. There will be a third 24" (60 cm) piece of wire remaining.

Step 2: Use one of the 26" (65 cm) wires to string 24 seed beads; slide them to the middle of the wire. Pass the wire through the donut. Pair the wire ends so the seed beads wrap around the donut.

Step 3: Keeping the wire ends paired, string 1 seamless round, one 6mm round, and 1 nugget.

Step 4: Separate the wires and use one wire end to string 1 seamless round. String 1 oval and one 8mm amethyst round ten times. String 5 seed beads, 1 crimp tube, and the bar half of the clasp. Pass back through the crimp tube and crimp.

Step 5: Using the other wire end, string 1 seamless round. String one 6mm round, one 8mm fluorite round, one 6mm round and 1 nugget five times. String 1 seamless round, 5 seed beads, 1 crimp tube, and the bar half of the clasp. Pass back through the crimp tube and crimp.

Step 6: Repeat Steps 2 through 5, this time using the other 26" (65 cm) piece of wire and attaching to the ring half of the clasp.

Step 7: Use the 24" (60 cm) piece of wire to string 24 seed beads; slide them to the middle of the wire. Pass the wire through the donut. Pair the wire ends so the seed beads wrap the donut between the 2 strands of seed beads already placed there.

Step 8: Keeping the wire ends paired, string 1 seamless round, one 6mm round, and 1 seamless round.

Step 9: Separate the wires and use one wire end to string 4 peridot chips, one 8mm amethyst round, 4 amethyst chips, and one 8mm amethyst round 5 times. String 5 seed beads, 1 crimp tube, and the bar half of the clasp so that this strand sits next to the one strung in Step 5. Pass back through the crimp tube and crimp.

Step 10: Repeat Step 8 using the other wire end and attaching to the ring half of the clasp.

RESOURCES
Stone chips, donut: Fire Mountain Gems.

Watermelon Slice

Anna Karena

A simple necklace design like this one is the perfect platform for featuring beautiful materials. The gradated tourmaline and sparkling crystals paired with the delicious slice of pink tourmaline are a feast for the eyes.

MATERIALS

174 green tourmaline 3mm Swarovski crystal bicones
6 green tourmaline 4mm Swarovski crystal bicones
12 rose satin 4mm Swarovski crystal bicones
80 pink tourmaline 4×6mm faceted ovals in graduated
   shades of color
1 pink tourmaline 12×16mm rough stone slice with
   1.5mm diamond inset
1 sterling silver 4mm soldered jump ring
8×12mm sterling silver lobster clasp
4 sterling silver 2mm crimp tubes
40" (100 cm) of .019 beading wire

TOOLS

Wire cutters
Chain-nose lpiers

FINISHED SIZE

18" (45 cm) (shortest strand)

Step 1: Attach 20" (51 cm) of beading wire to the clasp using a crimp tube.

Step 2: String 3 green 4mm bicones, 87 green 3mm bicones, the rough stone slice, 87 green 3mm bicones, 3 green 4mm bicones, 1 crimp tube, and the jump ring. Pass back through the tube and crimp.

Step 3: Attach 20" (51 cm) of beading wire to the clasp using a crimp tube.

Step 4: String 6 rose 4mm bicones, 80 tourmaline ovals (in gradating color), 6 rose 4mm bicones, 1 crimp tube, and the jump ring. Pass back through the tube and crimp.

RESOURCES

All materials: The Bead Monkey.

Dewdrops in the Grass

Tina Koyama

Mix as many colors and finishes into this bracelet as you like. Here, matte-finish dagger beads and sparkly fire-polished beads set off each other nicely.

MATERIALS
107 Czech pressed-glass 10–15mm daggers in 6 different sizes, colors, and finishes
46 Czech pressed-glass 7mm matte teardrops
9 Czech pressed-glass 8mm cubes
7 round 8mm Czech fire-polished beads
Sterling silver lobster clasp
6.5mm sterling silver soldered jump ring
6 sterling silver 2mm crimp tubes
30" (76 cm) of .014 beading wire

TOOLS
Crimping pliers
Wire cutters
Tape

FINISHED SIZE
7¼" (18 cm)

Step 1: Attach a 10" (25 cm) piece of wire to the soldered jump ring using a crimp tube. String 73 daggers, mixing 4 of the 6 kinds in the materials list. String 1 crimp tube and the lobster clasp. Pass back through the tube and crimp.

Step 2: Attach a 10" (25 cm) piece of wire to the soldered jump ring using a crimp tube. String 5 teardrops and 1 round. String 6 teardrops and 1 round six times. String 5 teardrops, 1 crimp tube, and the clasp. Pass back through the tube and crimp.

Step 3: Attach a 10" (25 cm) piece of wire to the soldered jump ring using a crimp tube. Mix up the other two types of daggers and string 3 or 4 of them followed by a cube. String 9 cubes total and end with 3 daggers. String 1 crimp tube and the clasp. Pass back through the tube and crimp.

RESOURCES
All materials: Fusion Beads.

Ferngirl

Paulette Livers

The colors and materials in this simple necklace—watery blue, grass green, and earthy stone—combine to create the effect of a dewy forest floor. Exposed gold beading wire imparts airy elegance, a nice foil to the heavy stone clasp.

MATERIALS

14 peridot 3mm rounds
13 jasper 4mm rounds
9 cane glass 7.5mm cubes
Polished 25×18mm rainforest jasper pillow
Fern-etched 28×40mm dichroic glass
   pendant
2 gold-filled 2mm crimp tubes
18" (45 cm) of .019 gold beading wire

TOOLS

Wire cutters
Crimping pliers

FINISHED SIZE

14" (36 cm)

Step 1: String 1 crimp tube and 1 round jasper. Pass back through the tube, pull snug, and crimp the tube. String the jasper pillow.

Step 2: String 7 peridot and 1 round jasper. String 1 cube and 1 round jasper four times. String the pendant and 1 round jasper. String 1 cube and 1 round jasper four times. String 7 peridot.

Step 3: String 1 crimp tube, 1 round jasper, 1 cube, and 1 round jasper. Pass back through the cube, the round jasper, and the tube to form a loop at the end of the wire. Adjust the size of the loop to fit over the jasper pillow at the other end of the wire, then crimp the tube.

RESOURCES

Cane glass: David Christensen; polished rainforest jasper: Avian Oasis; pendant: The Moontide Workshop.

(Red) Gold and Green

Dustin Wedekind

Because the beautifully striated turquoise focal bead in this necklace hardly needs embellishment, Dustin has chosen low-key green seed beads mixed with gold daisy spacers to complement the stone, like a chameleon in the grass.

MATERIALS

Hank of size 8° seed beads
2 round 4mm garnet beads
25×30mm turquoise bead
81 gold 4mm daisy spacers
2 gold 9×28mm cones
Gold toggle clasp
2 gold split rings
Two 4" (10 cm) pieces of 22-gauge gold wire
Spool of Dandyline stringing thread

TOOLS

Wire cutters
Round-nose pliers
Scissors
Size 10 beading needle

FINISHED SIZE

17" (43 cm)

Step 1: Use round-nose pliers to form a ¼" (.64 cm) wrapped loop at one end of each wire. Pull 6' of thread from the spool and pass through one of the wire loops. Without cutting the thread from the spool, tie a knot placing the wire near the spool.

Step 2: String 4½" (11 cm) of seed beads, 3 spacers, 2" (5 cm) of seed beads, the focal bead, 2" (5.08 cm) of seed beads, 3 spacers, and 4½" (11 cm) of seed beads. Pass through the second wire loop, pull the beads snug, and tie a knot.

Step 3: Repeat Step 2 ten times, placing the 3 spacers randomly once or twice among each strand of seed beads and passing back through the focal bead. End your working thread when it is shorter than the length of the necklace by passing back through one of the strands for a couple of inches, tying knots between beads, and trimming close. Pull another length of thread from the spool and cut the thread to finish stringing.

Step 4: String 1 cone and 1 garnet on a wire and form a wrapped loop. Use a split ring to attach the wrapped loop to one side of the clasp. Repeat on the other side of the necklace.

RESOURCES

Cones and clasp: Bead Cache.

Slow and Steady Wins

Jean Campbell

You don't see gold and turquoise paired too often in modern jewelry, but this color scheme was a favorite with the ancient Egyptians as well as those who subscribed to Rococo.

MATERIALS

1 turquoise 6mm round

32 turquoise 7mm faceted, diagonally drilled pillows

12 turquoise 6×9mm–7×10mm double-drilled faceted rectangles

20 vermeil 7×9mm flower beads

1 turquoise 30mm vegetable ivory button with shank

32 gold-filled 2mm crimp tubes

1 gold-filled 2" (5 cm) head pin

1 gold-filled 8mm soldered jump ring

Gold-filled 8×12mm lobster clasp

30" (76 cm) of gold-plated 8mm oval chain

192" (5 m) of 24k gold .019 beading wire

TOOLS

Wire cutters

Chain-nose pliers

Flat-nose pliers

Round-nose pliers

Crimping pliers

FINISHED SIZE

18" (45 cm) (including chain extender)

Step 1: Make sixteen 7-link pieces of chain and one 16-link piece. Set aside.

Step 2: String 1 flower and the round on the head pin and form a wrapped loop that attaches to the end of the 16-link chain. Set the chain extender aside.

Step 3: Cut sixteen 12" (30 cm) pieces of beading wire and set aside.

Step 4: Attach one of the beading wire pieces to the lobster clasp using a crimp tube. Repeat to attach 8 wires in all to the clasp. Set it aside.

Step 5: Repeat Step 2, attaching the remaining 8 wires to the soldered ring.

Step 6: Gather 4 wires on the soldered ring and string 1 flower. Gather the remaining 4 wires and string 1 flower. *String 1 square on each wire. Gather 4 wires and string 1 flower, making sure to rearrange the wires slightly so that you aren't gathering the same 4 wires as before. Repeat from * and set aside.

Step 7: Repeat Step 6 to string the clasp wires.

Step 8: Pair all 16 wires from both sides of the necklace and pass as many as possible through the button's shank.

Step 9: Gather the outer 4 wires on the left side of the button and string 1 flower. Repeat for the right side of the button. Gather the center 4 wires and string 1 flower. (There will be 4 unstrung wires in all.)

Step 10: Skipping the 2 outside left wires, gather the 2 wires extending from the flower and the next 2 wires; string 1 flower. Repeat for the right side of the button. The result should look like a net.

Step 11: Gather the 2 outside left wires and string 1 flower. Repeat for the right side of the button.

Step 12: String the rectangles on the wires in a 2-row staggered design, making sure the fronts of the rectangles face forward. Place 5 rectangles on the first row, and 7 on the second.

Step 13: String 1 crimp tube on each wire. Pass through the fourth link on one of the 7-link pieces of chain and back through the tube. Do not crimp. Repeat for all the wires.

Step 14: Adjust the beads and wires to make a pleasing design. Adjust the crimp tubes to accommodate any changes; crimp.

Step 15: Attach the chain extender to the soldered ring, placing it opposite the crimp tubes.

RESOURCES

Tagua button: On the Surface; turquoise: vermeil: Whole Bead; clasp: Fire Mountain Gems; chain: Ornamental Resources; beading wire: Soft Flex Company.

California Dreaming

Lea Worcester

Lea believes that people who grow up on or near the Pacific Coast will always be linked to the sight, smell, feel, and ambient sound of the ocean. This bracelet is one way that beach lovers can keep the sea close to them, no matter where they are.

MATERIALS

3 coral 6mm rondelles
10 assorted 8–10mm beads (Swarovski crystals, Czech glass, abalone shell, aventurine, and/or crackle glass beads)
3 aquamarine 12×18mm nuggets
12×16mm coral barrel bead
7" (18 cm) flat oval sterling silver chain
5 sterling silver beach-themed charms
Sterling silver 16mm lobster clasp
14 sterling silver 18-gauge 6mm jump rings
8mm soldered 18-gauge sterling silver jump ring
18" (46 cm) of 24-gauge sterling silver wire
12" (30.5 cm) of 18-gauge sterling silver wire
6" (15 cm) of 20-gauge sterling silver wire

TOOLS

Round-nose pliers
Chain-nose pliers
Wire cutters
Ruler
Beading mat

FINISHED SIZE

7¾" (20 cm)

TIP

Before you start any wirework, arrange the beads and chain on a mat to get an idea of where you want to attach them. The coral barrel and aquamarine beads lie horizontally on the chain; they don't hang down vertically.

Step 1: Use 6mm jump rings to attach the lobster clasp to one end of the chain and the 8mm soldered ring to the other end.

Step 2: Use 4" (10 cm) of 18-gauge wire to string 1 aquamarine bead and form a wrapped loop on each side of the bead. Repeat twice to make three links. Form a simple loop at one end of a 6" (15 cm) piece of 20-gauge wire. String the coral barrel, then wrap the wire loosely around to the opposite end and form another loop. Use jump rings to attach each loop to the chain; space the beads evenly and include extra links between the loops so the chain is not tight around the bead.

Step 3: Form a tight spiral at the end of a 2" (5 cm) piece of 24-gauge wire. String 1 assorted bead and form a loop to attach the bead to a link of the chain. Repeat for a total of 6 assorted beads placed randomly along the chain.

Step 4: Attach 4 assorted beads to the chain as follows: Center 1 bead on a 2" (5 cm) piece of 24-gauge wire. Following the contour of the bead, bend one end of the wire all the way up to meet the opposite end of the wire where it was originally inserted. Bend the wire 90 degrees across the top of the bead and wrap tightly around the stem 2 times; cut off excess. Form a wrapped loop with the stem and attach the bead to the chain before you close the wrap.

RESOURCES

Charms, lobster clasp, chain, Swarovski crystal, and aquamarine: Sweet Beads; coral barrel, Czech glass, abalone shell, and aventurine bead: Cosecha Designs; crackle glass beads: Out on a Whim.

Darling Clementine

Danielle Fox

Bursting with colorful glass beads, this striking necklace will become an integral accessory to your summer wardrobe. The carved and painted shell pendant is attached to the strand of art glass beads with embroidery floss.

MATERIALS
18 art glass 10×18mm beads
50mm shell flower pendant
19 round 4mm corrugated silver beads
2 sterling silver 2mm crimp tubes
Sterling silver toggle clasp
18" (46 cm) of .019 beading wire
Embroidery floss in colors to complement beads

TOOLS
Wire cutters
Crimping pliers
Scissors

FINISHED SIZE
16½" (42 cm)

Step 1: Attach the wire to one half of the clasp using a crimp tube.

Step 2: String 1 silver and 1 glass bead eighteen times. String 1 silver, 1 crimp tube, and the other half of the clasp. Pass back through the tube and crimp.

Step 3: Tie the pendant to the clasp with four to six 3" (8 cm) pieces of embroidery floss.

RESOURCES
Silver beads: Desert Gems.

Hot Summer Flowers

Kate McKinnon

MATERIALS
36 yellow Delica beads
21 rust size 11° seed beads
18 hot pink size 8° seed beads
31 metallic copper size 8° seed beads
12 vintage 3×8mm green glass daggers
23 fine silver spikes
6 lampworked 18–20mm flower beads
Fine silver toggle clasp
18 silver 2" head pins
9" (23 cm) of .024 beading wire

TOOLS
Round-nose pliers
Flat-nose pliers
Crimping pliers
Flush cutters

FINISHED SIZE
7½" (19 cm)

This is a beaded interpretation of Kate's garden in summer: lots of hot reds, pinks, oranges, and golds. Big fat rudbeckia and gerbera daisies and red poppies. Golden grasses and spiky butterfly bush flowers.

Step 1: String 4 Delicas and 1 hot pink size 8° onto a head pin and form a wrapped loop. Repeat eight times.

Step 2: String 3 size 11°s and 1 hot pink size 8° onto a head pin and form a wrapped loop dangle. Repeat six times.

Step 3: Attach the beading wire to one side of the clasp using a crimp tube. String 4 spikes, 1 Delica dangle, and 1 size 11° dangle. String 1 Delica dangle, 1 copper seed bead, 1 dagger, 1 flower, 1 dagger, 1 copper seed bead, 1 size 11° dangle, 1 copper seed bead, 1 spike, 1 copper seed bead, 1 spike, 1 copper seed bead, 1 spike, and 1 copper seed bead five times.

Step 4: String 1 Delica dangle, 1 copper seed bead, 1 dagger, 1 flower, 1 dagger, 1 Delica dangle, 1 size 11° dangle, 1 Delica dangle, 4 spikes, 1 crimp tube, and the other side of the clasp. Pass back through the tube and crimp.

RESOURCES
Seed beads: Jane's Fiber and Beads or Beyond Beadery; handmade fine silver spikes and clasp: Kate McKinnon; lampworked beads: Michele Goldstein.

Rings of Fire

Gregory Ogden

This necklace has a mythic look, as if its fiery design could protect the wearer. Gregory assures us that, when worn, the necklace will enhance visible clarity and clairvoyance.

1" (2.5 cm) onto both ends. Fold the ends back and wrap them together with 2" (5 cm) of sterling wire to secure. Repeat entire step for the other half of the necklace.

RESOURCES

Toggle, Fire Fairy red bead blend, pewter rings, and red silk: Green Girl Studios. Carnelian, amber, and apple coral: MB Imports. Wood beads: Fire Mountain Gems and Beads. Sterling silver beads: Kamol (wholesale only).

MATERIALS

- 1 box Fire Fairy red bead blend (includes bugle beads, seed beads, sequins, stone chips, pearls, and Czech glass—about 40" (102 cm) of 2–8mm beads)
- 6 wood 6mm rounds
- 2 carnelian 9–12mm rounds
- 2 amber 6×8mm chunks
- 1 apple coral 9mm round
- 1 wood 8×12mm rondelle
- 4 sterling silver 3×8mm tubes
- 15mm pewter ring
- 15mm gold/brass ring
- 18×25mm pewter oval pendant
- Sterling silver toggle clasp
- 4 sterling silver 2mm crimp tubes
- 40" (102 cm) of red silk cord
- 4" (10 cm) of 22-gauge sterling silver wire
- 46" (117 cm) of .014 beading wire

TOOLS

- Wire cutters
- Chain-nose pliers
- Crimping pliers

FINISHED SIZE

16" (41 cm) (shortest strand)

Step 1: Attach 24" (61 cm) of beading wire to one half of the clasp using a crimp tube. String 10" (25 cm) of red beads, the pewter ring, 10" (25 cm) of red beads, 1 crimp tube, and the other half of the clasp. Pass back through the tube and crimp.

Step 2: Attach 22" (56 cm) of wire to one half of the clasp using a crimp tube. String 8" (20 cm) of red beads, 1 amber, 1 apple coral, 1 wood rondelle, 1 carnelian, 1 amber, 1 carnelian, 8" (20 cm) of red beads, 1 crimp tube, and the other half of the clasp. Pass back through the tube and crimp.

Step 3: Slide the gold/brass ring down over the bar half of the clasp onto the strands of beads.

Step 4: Attach 20" (51 cm) of silk cord to the pewter oval using a lark's head knot so that you have two 10" (25 cm) ends. Use both ends to string 1 wood round. Use 1 end to string 1 tube. Use both ends to string 1 wood round. Use 1 end (the one not already used) to string 1 tube. Use both ends to string 1 wood. String one half of the clasp

Firecracker

Lindsay Burke

Named for the explosion of crystals on this bracelet, as well as for Lindsay's personality, this sumptuous bracelet is a blaze of elegance as it detonates on your wrist.

Step 1: Use a head pin to string 2 Siam and form a wrapped loop that attaches to the center link of the chain. Working toward one end of the chain, attach a 2-bead dangle to each link, gradating the colors as follows: Siam, light Siam satin, light Siam, hyacinth satin, hyacinth, and Indian red. Work 1-bead dangles to the end of the chain using sun, light peach, silk, and then clear. Repeat for the other half of the chain.

Step 2: Repeat Step 1 three times for a total of four 1- to 2-bead dangles per link. Work back from either end to attach a total of six light-color dangles per link.

Step 3: Use two jump rings to attach one half of the toggle to one end of the chain. Repeat for the other side.

RESOURCES

All materials: Fusion Beads.

MATERIALS

12 clear 3mm Swarovski crystal bicones
12 clear 4mm Swarovski crystal bicones
12 silk 4mm Swarovski crystal bicones
8 light peach 4mm Swarovski crystal bicones
12 sun 4mm Swarovski crystal bicones
16 hyacinth satin 4mm Swarovski crystal bicones
20 Indian red 4mm Swarovski crystal bicones
16 light Siam 4mm Swarovski crystal bicones
16 light Siam satin 4mm Swarovski crystal bicones
8 light peach 5mm Swarovski crystal bicones
20 hyacinth 5mm Swarovski crystal bicones
36 Indian red 5mm Swarovski crystal bicones
16 light Siam 5mm Swarovski crystal bicones
32 light Siam satin 5mm Swarovski crystal bicones
14 Siam 5mm Swarovski crystal bicones
16 light Siam satin 6mm Swarovski crystal bicones
4 Siam 6mm Swarovski crystal bicones
6 Siam 8mm Swarovski crystal bicones
12 Siam 6×9mm Swarovski crystal teardrops
6½" (16.5 cm) of 6mm gold-filled cable chain
4 gold-filled 3×5mm jump rings
Vermeil toggle clasp
186 gold-filled 24-gauge head pins

TOOLS

Round-nose pliers
Chain-nose pliers
Wire cutters

FINISHED SIZE

7" (18 cm)

NOTE

Colors are evenly gradated throughout the bracelet, so combine different sizes of the same color for the majority of the piece and combine different colors when the crystals blend from one color to another.

Lazy Jane Chain

Katie Wall

This playful piece reminds Katie of the long lazy days of her childhood. With the skin-tingling pink, amber, and yellow hues of Swarovski crystals, a variety of crystal shapes, and a large flat curb chain, she gives a new spin to the common wire-wrapped necklace.

Step 1: Using 6" (15 cm) of 22-gauge wire, form a wrapped loop on one side of the clasp. String 1 crystal and form a wrapped loop that attaches the clasp to one end of the chain. Repeat for the other side of the clasp.

Step 2: String 1 crystal on a head pin. Form a wrapped loop that attaches the pin to one link of the chain. Selecting crystals at random, repeat to attach 1 crystal to each link of the chain.

TIP

Swarovski crystals can get pricey. For a budget-conscious necklace, use various sizes and colors of seed beads or Czech glass.

RESOURCES

All materials: Fusion Beads.

MATERIALS

25 assorted 3–6mm topaz Swarovski crystal rounds, bicones, rondelles, and cubes
30 assorted 3–6mm light topaz Swarovski crystal rounds, bicones, rondelles, and cubes
30 assorted 3–6mm padparadscha Swarovski crystal rounds, bicones, rondelles, and cubes
Sterling silver daisy clasp
83 sterling silver 2" (5 cm) head pins
18" (46 cm) of sterling silver cable chain
12" (30.5 cm) of 22-gauge sterling silver wire

TOOLS

Chain-nose pliers
Round-nose pliers
Wire cutters

FINISHED SIZE

18½" (47 cm)

Indian Summer

Terry Rhoades

MATERIALS

- 7 agate 3mm heishis
- 2 green 6mm glass bicones
- 2 red 4×8mm glass ovals
- 3 carnelian 7×12mm bicones
- 4 jasper 8×12mm ovals
- 5 lampworked 14mm beads
- 14×20mm lampworked oval
- 24×32mm flat oval lampworked focal bead
- 75mm sterling silver tube with 5 loops
- 2 sterling silver charms
- 2 sterling silver beads
- Fancy sterling silver head pin
- 2 sterling silver 2" head pins
- 6" (5 cm) of sterling silver 24-gauge wire
- 30" (15 cm) of flat suede leather or faux suede
- 10" (25 cm) of beading wire
- 4 sterling silver 2mm Twisted Tornado crimp tubes

TOOLS

- Scissors
- Flat-nose pliers
- Round-nose pliers
- Wire cutters

FINISHED SIZE

18" (46 cm)

This necklace is a perfect addition to a casual outfit of jeans and a sweater. The silver tube with loops is a great showcase for art beads and fun charms.

Step 1: Use 4" (10 cm) of silver wire to form a wrapped loop that attaches to the center loop of the silver tube. String 1 glass bicone and the focal bead, then form a wrapped loop. Use a 3" (8 cm) wire to form a simple loop and attach it to the loop just made. String 1 jasper and form a simple loop. String 1 glass bicone on the fancy head pin and form a wrapped loop dangle that attaches to the simple loop just made.

Step 2: Attach 5" (13 cm) of beading wire to the next eye on the silver tube using a crimp tube. String 1 carnelian, 1 agate, 1 silver bead, 1 lampworked bead, 1 crimp tube, and 1 charm. Pass back through the tube and flatten. Repeat entire step on the other side of the focal bead, stringing 2 agate, 1 lampworked, 1 red glass, 2 agate, 1 silver, 1 agate, 1 crimp tube, and 1 charm.

Step 3: Use a head pin to string 1 jasper, 1 carnelian, and 1 jasper. Form a wrapped loop that attaches to an outside loop of the tube. Repeat for the other outside loop, stringing 1 carnelian, 1 jasper, 1 agate, and 1 red glass.

Step 4: Fold the leather cord in half and pass through the tube. Center the ends, with the folded end 1" (2.5 cm) shorter. Tie knots on each side of the tube to hold the leather in place. Tie another knot 2" (5 cm) from the tube on each side. Pass the looped side through the oval lampworked bead. Make another knot about 1" (2.5 cm) from the end to form a loop. Use the other ends of the leather cord to string 3 lampworked beads, then tie a knot at the end. Pull the last bead up to the knot and slip the bead through the loop on the other side to close the necklace.

RESOURCES

Lampworked beads: Steve Rhoades of Bokamo Designs; sterling silver tube: Rainbow Lodge; charms: Wynwoods Gallery & Bead Studio; silver beads, silver wire, and head pins: Rio Grande; Twisted Tornado crimp tubes: Via Murano.

Fall Fusion

Barbara Naslund

A fusion of colors and shapes sets off the lovely focal bead in this necklace. It's a great project for using up those cherished leftover beads in your stash.

MATERIALS

Size 11° Czech seed beads
200 assorted 2–6mm beads (pearls, fire-polished glass, semiprecious chips and round beads)
40mm 2-holed carved carnelian flower
2 Bali silver 8×12mm cones
Bali silver toggle clasp
2 sterling silver 2" (5 cm) eye pins
6 sterling silver 2mm crimp beads
120" (305 cm) of .014 beading wire

TOOLS

Wire cutters
Crimping pliers
Flat-nose pliers
Tape

FINISHED SIZE

15" (38 cm)

Step 1: Cut the wire into six 20" (51 cm) pieces.

Step 2: String one crimp tube on two wires. Pass the wires though the eye pin, back through the tube, and crimp. Repeat twice more with the other strands of wire.

Step 3: Randomly string beads on each strand until you get to the halfway mark. Make sure to space each assorted bead with 3–8 seed beads.

Step 4: String three stands of wire through each hole on the focal bead.

Step 5: Repeat Step 3 on the other side of the focal bead.

Step 6: Repeat Step 2.

Step 7: String 1 cone and 1 small bead on an eye pin. Forming a wrapped loop, attach the eye pin to one side of the clasp. Repeat for the other side of the necklace.

RESOURCES

Carved carnelian flower: Gems Resources Enterprise Inc. (wholesale only); Bali silver clasp and cones, eye pins, crimp beads, and beading wire: Bead Cache.

Cinnamon Green Tea

Rebecca Campbell

The rich colors of leaves, the nip in the air, the cozy corner by the fire. What better to do on a chilly autumn day than sit down with a hot cup of tea and your favorite beads to create something that speaks to the colors of the season . . . like this two-strand necklace of unakite, red jasper, and hairpipe beads.

MATERIALS

29 round 8mm unakite beads
7 red jasper 15×20mm nuggets
18 lime green 4×25mm bone hairpipe beads
Sterling silver 2-strand clasp
4 sterling silver 2mm crimp tubes
34" (86 cm) of .019 beading wire

TOOLS

Wire cutters
Crimping pliers

FINISHED SIZE

16" (41 cm) (shortest strand)

Step 1: Attach 18" (46 cm) of wire to one half of the clasp using a crimp tube.

Step 2: String 1 unakite, 1 jasper, 1 unakite, and 1 hairpipe three times.

Step 3: String 3 unakite, 1 jasper, and 3 unakite. Repeat Step 2, reversing the sequence. String 1 crimp tube and the other half of the clasp. Pass back through the tube and crimp.

Step 4: Attach 16" (41 cm) of wire to the second hole of the clasp. String 1 hairpipe and 1 unakite eleven times. String 1 hairpipe, 1 crimp tube, and the other side of the clasp. Pass back through the tube and crimp.

RESOURCES

All materials: Fire Mountain Gems and Beads.

Tibetan Melody

Christina Kline

MATERIALS
156 olive size 11° seed beads
44 red size 10° seed beads
4 silver-lined crystal size 6° seed beads
3 olive green 6×9mm ceramic rondelles
4 rosewood 5×7mm saucers
9 red coral 6mm rounds
3 wooden–4×22mm cylinders
7 white bone beads in assorted shapes and sizes
3 serpentine–20×24mm faceted flat ovals
2 patterned brown/white bone 24mm 1-hole
   round buttons
15 sterling silver twisted bugles
1 Hill tribe sterling silver 5×7mm horizontally
   drilled tube with flower design
7 silver 7×12mm Indian brass bells
2 sterling silver 2mm crimp tubes
36" (90 cm) of .019 beading wire

TOOLS
Wire cutters
4 Bead Stoppers
Crimping pliers

FINISHED SIZE
7¾" (19 cm)

RESOURCES
Coral: Fire Mountain Gems. Bone: Orr's Trading Post.
Wooden beads: Bobby Bead.

Y**ou** might spy a local wearing this eclectic multistranded bracelet as you stroll through a Tibetan marketplace.

Step 1: Cut two 18" (45 cm) pieces of beading wire. Put the ends together and string 45 olive size 11°s. Slide the seed beads to the center of the wires.

Step 2: Put all four wire ends together and string the silver tube. Slide it down the wires until it touches the seed beads, so the beads make a loop.

Step 3: Use one of the wires to string a random strand of beads and bells 6" (15 cm) long. End the strand with at least 7 seed beads. Clip a Bead Stopper to the end of the strand. Repeat for each of the remaining strands.

Step 4: Remove the Bead Stoppers from 2 of the strands. Pair the wire ends and string on 1 crimp tube, 1 size 6°, 1 button (from back to front), and 1 size 6°. Pass back through the button, the first size 6°, and the crimp tube. Snug the beads and crimp. Repeat for the remaining 2 strands.

Dragon Summer

Heather Culhane

This necklace plays host to whimsical glass beads, several different shapes of crystals, and Thai silver beads. Make the piece your own by stringing the flower charms in any order you please.

MATERIALS

- 4 chalcedony 4mm pink rondelles
- 11 fuchsia 4mm Swarovski crystal bicones
- 16 fuchsia 6mm Swarovski crystal bicones
- 2 violet opal 8mm Swarovski crystal cubes
- 3 faceted 8mm garnet rondelles
- 3 lampworked 9mm glass beads
- 4 flat tabular 20mm lampworked glass beads
- 1 lampworked 18×45mm glass bead with frog
- 9 Thai silver 4mm cornerless cubes
- 13 Thai silver 4mm coiled beads
- 18 Thai silver 4mm pyramids
- 4 Thai silver 8mm cubes
- 5 Thai silver 8mm snowflake spacers
- 5 assorted 4–8mm Thai silver beads and spacers
- 10 Thai silver 25mm flower charms
- 4 Thai silver 18mm flower charms
- 2 Thai silver 20mm flower beads with 3 holes
- 1 Thai silver 40mm dragonfly charm
- 1 Thai silver 60mm dragonfly pendant
- 8 round 10mm Thai silver pillow beads
- 2 round 18mm Thai silver hammered coins
- 1 sterling silver 32mm S-hook clasp
- 2 sterling silver 7mm split rings
- 2 sterling silver 8mm jump rings
- 3" (8 cm) of sterling silver chain
- 4 sterling silver 2mm crimp tubes
- 48" (122 cm) of .019 beading wire

TOOLS

Wire cutters
Crimping pliers

FINISHED SIZE

23" (58 cm)

Step 1: Attach two 24" (61 cm) pieces of wire to a split ring using 2 crimp tubes.

Step 2: Hold both wires together and string 1 cornerless cube and one 10mm pillow four times. String one 4mm crystal, one 18mm hammered coin, 1 coiled bead, and 1 tabular lampworked bead.

Step 3: Separate the strands and string ½" (1 cm) of beads and flower charms. Pass the wires in opposite directions through one hole of the 3-hole flower bead. String ½" (1 cm) of beads on each wire, then pass one wire through each of the other two holes of the 3-hole flower. Hold the strands together and string 1 tabular lampworked bead.

Step 4: Separate the strands and string 2" (5 cm) of beads and flowers onto each strand. Hold the strands together and string the large dragonfly, one 6mm bicone crystal, the lampworked frog bead, and one 6mm bicone crystal. Separate the strands and string ½" (1 cm)) of beads and charms. Hold the strands together and string 1 tabular lampworked bead.

Step 5: Repeat Steps 3 to 1 for the other half of the necklace.

Step 6: Use 8mm jump rings to attach the chain to one of the split rings and the small dragonfly to the end of the chain. Pass each side of the S-hook through a split ring.

Electric Light

Lindsay Burke

In this piece bold strips of color create the climate of a hot summer day. Combining smooth round pearls and angled bicone crystals, Lindsay's innovative bracelet is an amazingly simple way to achieve an electric effect.

MATERIALS

50 fuchsia 4mm Swarovski crystal bicones
50 padparadscha 4mm Swarovski crystal bicones
50 lime 4mm Swarovski crystal bicones
50 ruby 4mm Swarovski crystal bicones
36 lime 5mm freshwater pearls
25 melon 7mm freshwater pearls
23 red 6mm freshwater pearls
28 fuchsia 6mm freshwater pearls
Sterling silver four-strand tube clasp
16 sterling silver 2mm crimp tubes
6' (183 cm) of .014 beading wire

TOOLS

Wire cutters
Crimping pliers

FINISHED SIZE

7½" (19 cm)

Step 1: Cut the wire into eight equal lengths. Attach two wires to each loop on one half of the clasp using crimp tubes.

Step 2: String one type of bead on one wire. String a crimp tube, pass through the corresponding loop on the other half of the clasp, then pass back through the tube and crimp. Repeat for each type of bead.

RESOURCES

All materials: Fusion Beads.

TIP

Create texture within a strand by using more than one bead type.

Lascaux

Dustin Wedekind

Like drawings in an ancient cave, the lines in this glass pendant are echoed by the earthly scribblings in the jasper beads. When worn, the silver tubes transform the wearer into an animal in a mystic hunt.

MATERIALS

1 garnet 3.5mm faceted round
6 jasper 6mm rounds
10 picture jasper 30mm coins
Lampworked glass and PMC 16×60mm focal bead
20 sterling silver 2.5mm rounds
2 Thai silver 6×45mm curved tubes
Sterling silver toggle clasp
2 sterling silver 2×3mm crimp tubes
28" (71 cm) of .019 beading wire

TOOLS

Wire cutters
Crimping pliers

FINISHED SIZE

19½" (49.5 cm)

Step 1: String the garnet to the center of the wire. Use both ends together to string the focal bead.

Step 2: Use one end of the wire to string 3 silver rounds, 1 jasper round, 1 silver tube, 1 jasper round, and 1 silver round. String 1 jasper coin and 1 silver round five times. String 1 jasper round, 1 silver round, 1 crimp tube, and one half of the clasp. Pass back through the tube and crimp.

Step 3: Repeat Step 2 with the other end of the wire.

RESOURCES

Focal bead: Zoa Art. Jasper coins: Dakota Enterprises. Silver tubes and toggle: Saki Silver.

Sunset in Kyoto

Elizabeth Chumtong

MATERIALS
24 Thai silver 14mm coins
7 Thai silver 3mm rounds
Oversized 22k gold-plated toggle clasp
2 sterling silver 2mm crimp tubes
24" (61 cm) of .024 beading wire
TOOLS
Wire cutters
Crimping pliers
FINISHED SIZE
16" (41 cm)

The inspiration for this piece is the fabulously large gold toggle that serves as both pendant and clasp. Mixing metals and finishes has been one of Elizabeth's recent interests, hence the matte-finish silver beads and the shiny gold centerpiece.

Step 1: Attach the wire to the round half of the toggle clasp using a crimp tube.

Step 2: String one 3mm bead, the silver coins, six 3mm beads, 1 crimp tube, and the other half of the clasp. Pass back through the tube and crimp. Make sure the wire is not pulled too tight because the disk beads can be inflexible when they're not spaced out by smaller beads.

RESOURCES
All materials: Saki Silver.

Grace

Lindsay Burke

Lindsay needed new jewelry for autumn, so she created this chic bracelet. It reminds her of something that Grace Kelly would have worn in *To Catch a Thief*, in which she played a wealthy temptress whose heart of gold matched her riches. No wonder she captivated the former jewel thief played by Cary Grant.

MATERIALS

11 round 6mm garnet Swarovski crystals
11 light Colorado topaz 6mm Swarovski crystal cubes
7 round 8mm garnet Swarovski crystals
5 8mm light Colorado topaz Swarovski crystal cubes
11 round 8mm bronze Swarovski pearls
11 round 8mm brown Swarovski pearls
7 round 10mm bronze Swarovski pearls
7 round 10mm brown Swarovski pearls
Sterling silver toggle
70 sterling silver 24-gauge head pins
2 sterling silver 6mm jump rings
6½" (16.5 cm) of sterling silver cable chain

TOOLS

Round-nose pliers
Chain-nose pliers
Wire cutters

FINISHED SIZE

7" (18 cm)

Step 1: String 1 bead onto a head pin and form a wrapped loop that attaches to one link of the chain. Repeat for the length of the chain, making sure that the placement of bead types is random.

Step 2: Repeat Step 1, placing a second bead on every other link of the chain, or until all the beads are used.

Step 3: Use jump rings to attach one half of the toggle to each end of the chain.

RESOURCES

All materials: Fusion Beads.

Hail to the Queen!

Katie Wall

Katie wanted to create a piece of jewelry that would make her feel like royalty when she wore it. With its three strands of toasty brown and gold-toned crystals and pearls, this necklace fits the bill.

MATERIALS

- 182 dark brown size 15° seed beads
- 105 light Colorado topaz 3mm Swarovski crystal bicones
- 69 round 3mm copper Swarovski pearls
- 66 smoky topaz 4mm Swarovski crystal bicones
- 21 round 4mm copper Swarovski pearls
- 47 light Colorado topaz 13×6.5mm Swarovski crystal teardrops
- 180 silver-plated 3mm daisy spacers
- Sterling silver 3-strand clasp
- 6 sterling silver 2mm crimp tubes
- 54" (137 cm) of .014 beading wire

TOOLS

- Wire cutters
- Crimping pliers

FINISHED SIZE

16½" (42 cm)

Step 1: Cut the wire into three 18" (46 cm) pieces. Attach one end of each wire to one half of the clasp using crimp tubes.

Step 2: Use an outer wire to string 1 size 15°, 1 spacer, one 3mm pearl, 1 spacer, 1 size 15°, and five 3mm bicones twenty-one times. String 1 crimp tube and the other half of the clasp. Pass back through the tube and crimp.

Step 3: Use the center wire to string three 4mm bicones, 1 size 15°, 1 spacer, one 4mm pearl, 1 spacer, and 1 size 15° twenty-one times. String three 4mm bicones, 1 crimp tube, and the other half of the clasp. Pass back through the tube and crimp.

Step 4: Use the other outer wire to string 1 size 15°, 1 daisy spacer, one 3mm pearl, 1 daisy spacer, 1 size 15° seed bead, and 1 teardrop forty-seven times. String 1 spacer, 1 pearl, 1 spacer, 1 size 15°, and 1 crimp tube. Pass back through the tube and crimp.

RESOURCES

All materials: Fusion Beads.

Helena

SaraBeth Cullinan

T his necklace, like the Greek belly dancer it is named for, is subtle, flirty, elegant, and timeless. Opa!

MATERIALS

52 Moss mix 3mm Swarovski crystal bicones (14 jonquil, 14 lime, 8 light olivine, and 16 olivine)

49 Moss mix 6mm Swarovski crystal bicones (11 jonquil, 18 lime, 8 light olivine, and 12 olivine)

124 khaki 3×5mm freshwater pearls

60 brass 3mm rounds

Antique gold pewter and rhine-stone hook-and-eye clasp

2 antique gold pewter 5-to-1 flower design connectors

14 gold-filled 2mm crimp tubes

65" (165 cm) of .014 beading wire

TOOLS

Wire cutters

Crimping pliers

FINISHED SIZE

19½" (49.5 cm)

Step 1: Use crimp tubes to attach each strand to each successive loop of the connectors, stringing the strands as follows:

Strand 1: Use 9" (23 cm) of wire to string 1 brass, 31 pearls, and 1 brass.

Strand 2: Use 9½" (24 cm) of wire to string 1 brass. String one 3mm crystal and 1 pearl twenty-three times. String one 3mm crystal and 1 brass.

Strand 3: Use 10" (25 cm) of wire to string 1 brass and one 6mm crystal twenty-one times. String 1 brass.

Strand 4: Use 10½" (27 cm) of wire to string 1 brass. String one 3mm crystal and 1 pearl twenty-seven times. String one 3mm crystal and 1 brass.

Strand 5: Use 11" (28 cm) of wire to string 1 brass, 43 pearls, and 1 brass.

Step 2: Attach 7½" (19 cm) of wire to the top loop of one connector. String 1 brass and one 6mm crystal fourteen times. String 1 brass, 1 crimp tube, and one half of the clasp. Pass back through the tube and crimp. Repeat entire step with the other connector and second half of the clasp.

RESOURCES

All findings and freshwater pearls: Shipwreck Beads. Moss Swarovski crystal mixes: Beyond Beadery. Brass rounds: Rio Grande.

TIP
Make your own crystal mixes or purchase pre-mixed crystals to experiment with different color combinations.

Sediment

Liz Jones

MATERIALS
204 blue/green size 11° Japanese seed beads
90 khaki 3mm Swarovski crystal bicones
64 smoky topaz 4mm Swarovski crystal bicones
52 moss agate 4mm rounds
50 wood 5mm rounds
11 wood 4×8mm rondelles
11 Tahitian blue 12mm Swarovski glass pearls
22 sterling silver 5mm twisted heishi spacers
Ceramic 50mm pendant
2 sterling silver 10×30mm cones
1 sterling silver 18mm soldered ring
sterling silver hook-and-eye leaf clasp
8 sterling silver 2mm crimp tubes
4 sterling silver crimp covers
12" (30.5 cm) of 22-gauge sterling silver wire
72" (183 cm) of .014 beading wire

TOOLS
Round-nose pliers
Chain-nose pliers
Crimping pliers
Wire cutters
Bead Stoppers

FINISHED SIZE
21½" (55 cm)

Natural rock formations seen on a recent trip to the western United States inspired this timeless necklace. The earthy tones and natural materials mimic the colorful layers of soil and sediment found in those formations.

Step 1: Use 4" (10 cm) of 22-gauge wire to form a wrapped loop. Repeat once. Use 4" (10 cm) of 22-gauge wire to form a wrapped loop that attaches to the pendant; string one 4mm bicone and form a wrapped loop that attaches to the soldered ring. Set aside.

Step 2: Use 12" (30.5 cm) of beading wire to string 1 crimp tube, 9 seed beads, and the ring. Pass back through the tube and crimp. Cover the tube with a crimp cover.

Step 3: String 1 spacer, 1 rondelle, 1 spacer, and 1 pearl eleven times. String 1 crimp tube and one of the wrapped loops. Pass back through the tube and crimp. Use the wrapped-loop wire to string 1 cone and form a wrapped loop that attaches to one half of the clasp.

Step 4: Use two 12" (30.5 cm) pieces of wire to string 1 crimp tube. String 9 seed beads on each wire. Pass both wires through the ring and back through the tube; crimp and cover. Repeat once, then repeat Step 2, for a total of five wires.

Step 5: Use each strand of wire to string all of one type of remaining bead, placing a Bead Stopper at the end of the wires. Braid the strands together, then attach each one to the second wrapped loop using a crimp tube. Use the wrapped loop wire to string 1 cone and form a wrapped loop that attaches to the other half the clasp.

RESOURCES
Ceramic pendant: Marsha Neal Studio. All materials: Fusion Beads.

Spirit Sent

Jean Campbell

This substantial piece features banana-leaf beads, amazonite, and Mexican "miracle" charms, or *milagros*. Putting it on instantly brings one to another time, another place.

MATERIALS

2 bronze 4mm wooden rounds
12 mottled tan 7mm vintage rounds
113 amazonite 8mm chips
24 amazonite 6×10mm rondelles
11 banana leaf 21mm rounds
6 African brass 5×7mm tubes
26 brass 10×25mm milagros or other type of charms
20×44mm brass hand charm
African brass 32mm cross with 4 holes
Brass swan clasp
26 gold 2" (5 cm) eye pins
1 gold 3" (7.5 cm) eye pin
87 gold 2" (5 cm) head pins
11 gold 6.5mm 18-gauge jump rings
4 gold 2mm crimp tubes
Hypo Cement (optional)
30" (75 cm) of .019 beading wire

TOOLS

Wire cutters
Chain-nose pliers
Round-nose pliers
Crimping pliers

FINISHED SIZE

18" (45 cm)

Step 1: String 1 chip on 1 head pin and form a wrapped loop. Repeat to make 87 short dangles in all.

Step 2: String 12 of the short dangles on 1 jump ring. Repeat to make 7 short dangle clusters in all. (You will have 3 short dangles left over.) Set all aside.

Step 3: String 1 chip on one 2" (5 cm) eye pin and form a wrapped loop. Open the eye and add a small charm. Repeat to make 26 long dangles in all.

Step 4: String 12 of the long dangles on 1 jump ring. Repeat to make 2 long dangle clusters in all. (You will have 2 long dangles left over). Set all aside.

Step 5: Open 1 jump ring and string on 3 short dangles, the 3" (7.5 cm) eye pin, and the hand charm.

Step 6: Use the 3" (7.5 cm) eye pin to string 1 rondelle, one 21mm round, 1 short dangle cluster, and 1 rondelle; form a simple loop. Attach the jump ring from Step 5 to the simple loop just made. Set this focal dangle aside.

Step 7: Attach 15" (37.5 cm) of beading wire to one half of the clasp using a crimp tube. String one 4mm round. String one 7mm round, 1 rondelle, 1 brass tube, and 1 rondelle 3 times. String one 7mm round and 1 rondelle. String one 21mm round and 1 short dangle cluster 3 times. String one 21mm round, 1 rondelle, one 7mm round, the cross (diagonally), one 7mm round, 1 rondelle, one 21mm round, 1 rondelle, 1 long dangle cluster, 1 rondelle, 1 crimp tube, and 1 long dangle. Pass back through the crimp tube and crimp.

Step 8: Repeat Step 6 to make the other side of the necklace. Set aside.

Step 9: Open 1 jump ring and attach it to the loop that holds one of the small charms. Using the same jump ring, string the focal dangle and the loop that holds one of the small charms on the other side of the necklace. Close the ring.

Step 10: If needed, apply a small amount of glue to the 7mm rounds that surround the cross so they stay in place.

RESOURCES

Stones: Dakota Enterprises; Fire Mountain Gems; milagros: Glorianna's; banana leaf beads: The Bead Monkey.

Blue Ice Lariat

Margot Potter

The tiny seed beads between the larger beads in this lariat take on the look of knots, and the Swarovski crystals give the design super sparkle. But the stars of this necklace are the delicate ice blue cloisonné beads.

MATERIALS
129 aqua blue-lined size 14° seed beads
54 metallic silver 4mm Czech fire-polished beads
27 round 5mm Swarovski crystals
15 white 6mm freshwater pearls
26 Chinese cloisonné 7mm rounds
13 clear AB 8mm faceted Czech glass rounds
8×18mm clear AB Swarovski crystal teardrop
2 silver-plated 3mm crimp tubes
40" (102 cm) of .013 beading wire

TOOLS
Wire cutters
Crimping pliers
Round-nose pliers
Chain-nose pliers

FINISHED SIZE
35" (89 cm)

Step 1: Use the wire to string 1 crimp tube, 5 seed beads, the teardrop, and 5 seed beads. Pass back through the tube and crimp.

Step 2: String 1 pearl, 1 seed bead, 1 crystal, 1 seed bead, 1 fire-polished, 1 seed bead, and 1 fire-polished. String 1 cloisonné, 1 glass, 1 cloisonné, 1 fire-polished, 1 seed bead, 1 fire-polished, 1 seed bead, 1 crystal, 1 seed bead, 1 pearl, 1 seed bead, 1 crystal, 1 seed bead, 1 fire-polished, 1 seed bead, and 1 fire-polished thirteen times. String 1 seed bead, 1 pearl, 1 crimp tube, and 37 seed beads. Pass back through the tube and crimp.

RESOURCES
Fire-polished beads: Fusion Beads; crystals: Beyond Beadery; cloisonné beads: eebeads.com; wire and crimping tubes: Beadalon (wholesale only).

TIP
Display this simple, elegant lariat three ways: Wear it as a typical lariat; wear it as a short, two-strand necklace by wrapping it around your neck twice; or wear it as a bracelet by wrapping it around your wrist several times.

Kelli's Key West Fest

Krista Tseu

MATERIALS

1 Bermuda blue 6mm Swarovski crystal bicone
4 lampworked 7mm beads
6 borosilicate 9mm lampworked beads
10 abalone shell 20mm disks
16 Thai silver 4mm cornerless cubes
18 Thai silver 3×5mm rectangles
4 Thai silver 12mm starburst coins
2 Thai silver 18mm swirl coins
50mm Thai silver flower pendant
Large sterling silver toggle clasp
24-gauge sterling silver 2" (5 cm) head pin
2 sterling silver 2mm crimp tubes
24" (61 cm) of .019 beading wire

TOOLS

Wire cutters
Crimping pliers
Flat-nose pliers
Round-nose pliers

FINISHED SIZE

20" (51 cm)

This necklace captures the essence of a special sunny afternoon in Key West. You, too, can keep dreams and memories around your neck by stringing them into a beautiful piece of jewelry.

Step 1: Attach the wire to one half of the clasp using a crimp tube. String one 4mm, 1 rectangle, 1 abalone, one 4mm, one 7mm, one 4mm, 1 rectangle, 1 abalone, 1 rectangle, 1 starburst, 1 rectangle, 1 abalone, 1 rectangle, 1 swirl, 1 rectangle, 1 abalone, 1 rectangle, one 4mm, one 9mm, one 4mm, one 9mm, one 4mm, 1 rectangle, 1 abalone, 1 rectangle, 1 starburst, one 4mm, one 9mm, one 4mm, and one 7mm.

Step 2: String the flower pendant. Repeat Step 2, reversing the sequence.

Step 3: String the crystal onto the head pin and attach it to the ring side of the clasp by forming a wrapped loop.

RESOURCES

Borosilicate lampworked beads: Karl Tseu of 5 Fish Designs; abalone shell disks, crimp tubes, head pin, and toggle clasp: Rio Grande; Thai silver components: You & Me Silver.

Project Contributors

An avid Red Wings fan, **Annie Hartman Bakken** works out her frustrations of living in Avalanche Country by crafting.

Ruby Bayan is usually a writer first and a beadworker second but has lately been caught switching roles. She shares her writing and handcrafted jewelry through www.oursimplejoys.com.

Marlene Blessing is the editor of *Beadwork* magazine. A couple of years ago, she took a break from her long career as a trade book editor to return to her love of handcrafting. Now it's all in a day's work—and she couldn't be happier.

Lindsay Burke lives in Seattle with her husband, Andy, and her dog, Brutus. A beader since she was young, Lindsay teaches beading and works at Fusion Beads.

Jean Campbell is a craft author and editor whose specialty is beading. She is the founding editor of *Beadwork* magazine and has written and edited several books, including *The New Beader's Companion* (with Judith Durant), *Getting Started Stringing Beads*, and *Beaded Weddings* (all Interweave Press). Jean lives in Minneapolis, Minnesota with her family and a whole lot of beads.

Rebecca Campbell, managing editor of Interweave's book program, loves beading, knitting, cooking, reupholstering, and most other things that allow her to use her hands and be creative. But most of all she enjoys spending time with her two favorite guys, Greg and Turner, drinking red wine, and not bothering with dusting.

Elizabeth Chumtong owns Saki Silver with her husband Saki. She has been designing and selling silver beads and beadwork for twelve years. Contact Elizabeth at info@sakisilver.com or visit www.sakisilver.com.

Jenna Colyar-Cooper is an art history and photography student at Western Washington University and works at Fusion Beads in Seattle. She has been creating beaded jewelry for eight years.

Suzy Cox is co-founder of Shiny Bright Objects, a home-based jewelry design company. She has a 17-year career in marketing and advertising, and got bit by the beading bug a few years ago. She quickly became consumed. Contact Suzy at info@shinybrightobjects.com.

Heather Culhane of Red Ocean Jewellery Company is a London-based artist who makes unique pieces that contain handmade glass. She has been successful in her first year of selling her work and is represented in a gallery (www.artshed-ware.com) and at the London shop Dizar. To see Heather's fair schedule or more of her work, visit www.redocean.org.uk.

SaraBeth Cullinan divides her time between beading and belly dancing. She is a frequent contributor to *Beadwork* magazine. She can be reached at sarabeth44@ msn.com.

Abbie Enyart is an advertising executive extraordinaire who likes beads and margaritas. She lives in Loveland with her fatty kitty, her fugitive puppy, and her fisherman husband.

Kerry Flint became hooked on stringing after she assured her best friend, Bonnie Gorton, that they could make bracelets and earrings for Bonnie's upcoming wedding. And they did!

Danielle Fox is managing editor of *Beadwork* magazine. She fits in beading between reading, writing, and taking in the great Colorado outdoors.

Keriann Gore is a recent graduate of the apparel design program at Colorado State University. She is a frequent contributor to *Beadwork* and *Stringing* magazines and is now the manager of Bead Cache in Fort Collins, Colorado.

Bonnie Gorton became addicted to beading because of her "bestest" friend, Interweave Press's Kerry Flint. Bonnie is a banker by day and a beading junkie at night.

Regina Greer-Smith is the owner/designer of Send Us Your Ears (www.sendusyourears.com), a business that conducts classes at independent coffee shops through its Beans and Beads Institute.

Sara Hardin, a representative of Soft Flex Company, has a flair for designing exquisitely dainty jewelry. Following the philosophy of less is more, she keeps her creations simple and light to reflect her upbeat, optimistic personality.

Jamie Hogsett is editor of *Stringing* and special projects editor of *Beadwork* magazine. She works with beads, plays with beads, and lately inhales beads, as they are taking over her house.

Tamara Honaman, Media Content Manager for Fire Mountain Gems and Beads, is a jewelry designer, teaches classes at national jewelry and bead shows, is a regular guest on PBS's "Beads, Baubles & Jewels," has appeared on DIY's "Jewelry Making," and writes jewelry-making projects and industry-related articles. She has been making jewelry for over ten years, working in many different media.

Liz Jones recently moved to Seattle from Ohio. She works at Fusion Beads and eats, sleeps, and breathes beads.

Gail Kanemoto Hogsett is surrounded by gorgeous jewelry designs—both in her twenty-five years in the fine jewelry business and in witnessing the spectacular creations of her daughter, Jamie.

Anna Karena lives in Minneapolis, Minnesota and is the manager of a bead store. In her free time she enjoys taking ballet classes and performing in community theater as well as her new found addiction, hand spinning yarn. Contact her by e-mail at annakarena@mac.com.

Jaida Kimmerer works at a Montessori School and Fusion Beads. She owns her own jewelry/stationery business in Seattle, StrawBarry, named after her boyfriend.

Christina Kline is a bead artist who specializes in one-of-a-kind jewelry designs. Her innovative use of materials and keen eye for fashion account for her unique creations. Christina is an Executive Director of Shiny Bright Objects (www.shinybrightobjects.com), a home-based jewelry design company. She lives in Superior, Wisconsin with her husband and three children.

Tina Koyama is a beadwork artist, instructor, and writer who lives in Seattle, Washington. View Tina's beadwork at www.tinakoyama.com.

Laura Levaas lives in Thornton, Colorado, and is a key player on Interweave's book team. In her spare time, she makes a valiant effort to finish her knitting and beading projects.

Paulette Livers beads for fun and gift-giving. She's the Art Director of Interweave's book program.

Kate McKinnon is a self-taught bead and metal artist who teaches and exhibits internationally, and works out of her studio in her home town of Tucson, Arizona. She has authored two popular books on jewelry making and was the 2005 Rio Grande Saul Bell award winner for her PMC work. See more of her work including some beautiful variations of the Shag Carpet of Pearls, on her web site, www. katemckinnon.com.

Barbara Naslund says of beading: "What could be better than an afternoon filled with beautiful beads and your best buddies sitting around creating and challenging each other?" She is circulation manager at Interweave Press.

Greg Ogden has been working with Green Girl Studios for two years. When he's not making and selling beads, he spends his time writing, drawing, and playing music.

Margot Potter is a freelance writer, jewelry/project designer, and TV spokesperson. She resides outside Philadelphia with her husband Drew, daughter Avalon, and Cairn terrier Mrs. Fellerbee. Margot is currently working with North Light Press on a book that introduces beaded jewelry design to the technically and time-challenged crafter.

Carol Reesha has found all of her passions in the last three years: her husband, Vince, living in Carlsbad, California, and beading. Her website is www.CarolJeanDesigns.com.

Terry Rhoades started beading after her husband, Steve, began making borosilicate glass beads. After starting out with a tackle box of beads and findings, she now has a whole room devoted to beading! Terry and Steve live in Overland Park, Kansas, and have three grown children.

Terry Ricoli is a freelance designer, writer, and instructor living in the wine country of California. She also loves to combine beads with her needlepoint designs and home décor projects.

Maha Rizk came to the United States from Cairo, Egypt. She is the mother of two wonderful children and a research associate at a pharmaceutical company. Beading is her way to relax.

Candice Schneider lives in Minnetonka, Minnesota and works at The Bead Monkey. You can contact her at candiceschneider@yahoo.com.

Mike Sherman, owner of Soft Flex Company, is a top-notch designer who thinks outside the box. He has no limits or boundaries and will mix unusual colors and shapes to create exquisite jewelry.

Beth Simmons lives in Stormville, New York with six parrots and works as a secretary to support her beading habit. She has recently discovered polymer clay.

The **Thiens** are a part of the Karen community in Thailand. For years they have strived to share the villagers' hidden talents with the world.

Cynthia Thornton is a painter, sculptor, and lover of food. She lives in Asheville, North Carolina, with her husband, Greg, sister, Sheila, and daughter, Azalea.

Krista Tseu of 5 Fish Designs creates lampworked beads and jewelry designs with her husband (and co-glass artist), Karl. The couple has three daughters and lives in Virginia Beach, Virginia. Their glass art designs can be found at www.5fishdesigns.com.

Katie Wall has been a beadworker for twelve years. She works at Fusion Beads in Seattle.

Nancy Norden Walters discovered beads about twenty-two years ago. She owns Blue Frog Beads in Elmhurst, Illinois, where she lives with her husband, daughter, and four lucky cats.

Dustin Wedekind is senior editor of *Beadwork* magazine, where he is also known as Bead Boy. A seed-beader for over ten years, he finally succumbed to the "fancy beads" only recently.

Recently on PBS and HGTV, **Kristal Wick** invented Sassy Silkies, handpainted silk beads. She designs jewelry, teaches, and is writing *Sassy Silky Savvy*.

Lea Worcester teaches beading and wirework at Sweet Beads in Minnetonka, Minnesota, and is a certified Level One PMC instructor. E-mail her at leaworcester@mn.rr.com.

Julie Wood is currently a junior at Chapman University in California. She loves to bead, especially with her family, when she gets a break from school.

Karen Wood was introduced to beading when her niece sponsored a "beading day" for her office staff. Karen feels that beading is a "great bonding" activity.

Resources

2bead.com
13015 Compton Rd.
Loxahatchee, FL 33470
(877) 418-BEAD
www.tobead.com

ABC Direct
355 E. Ft. Lowell
Tucson, AZ 85705
(520) 696-0032
www.beadholiday.com

A&P Trading/House of Gems
(wholesale only)
607 S. Hill St., #8
Los Angeles, CA 90014
(213) 624-6280
www.houseofgems.com

Alexander's Bead Bazaar
6307 Roosevelt Wy. Northeast
Seattle, WA 98115
(206) 526-8909
www.alexandersbeads.com

Ands Silver
(323) 254-5250
www.andssilver.com

Anil Kumar
PO Box 3471
Fremont, CA 94539
(510) 498-8455

Applegate Lapidary
(209) 296-0929
www.applegatelapidary.com

Artgems
3850 E. Base Line Rd. Ste. 119
Mesa, AZ 85206
(480) 545-6009
www.artgemsinc.com

Avian Oasis
1644 N. 192 Ave.
Buckeye, AZ 85326
(602) 571-3385
www.avianoasis.com

Ayla's Originals
1511 Sherman Ave.
Evanston, IL 60201
(847) 328-4040
www.aylasoriginals.com

Barbara Becker Simon
122 SW 46th Terrace
Cape Coral, FL 33914
(239) 549-5971
www.bbsimon.com

Bead Bar
(407) 426-8826
www.beadbarbead.com

Bead Boss
www.beadboss.com
644 NW Highway
Cary, IL 60013
(847) 462-1522

Bead Cache
3307 S. College Ave.
Ft. Collins, CO 80525
(970) 224-4322

Bead Club
www.beadclub.com
(425) 949-1080

The Bead Goes On
(866) 861-2323
www.beadgoeson.com

The Bead Monkey
3717 W. 50th St.
Minneapolis, MN 55410
(952) 929-4032
www.thebeadmonkey.com

Bead Stopper Company
4939 E. Chestnut Dr.
Claremore, OK 74019
(918) 343-8905
www.beadstopper.com

Beadalon
(wholesale only)
205 Carter Dr.
West Chester, PA 19382
(800) 824-9473
www.beadalon.com

Bead Time
11570 S. Orange Blossom Trail
Ste. #13
Orlando, FL 32837
(407) 854-3515
www.bead-time.com

Beads and Beyond
25 102nd Avenue NE
Bellevue, WA 98804
(425) 462-8992

Beads U Need
640 S. Hill, #254
Los Angeles, CA 90014
(213) 622-9821
beadsuneed@yahoo.com

Beadstringers
7735 W. Long Dr., #14
Littleton, CO 80123
(303) 703-4679

Better Creation, Inc.
41-79 Gleane St.
Elmhurst, NY 11373
(718) 898-2788

Beyond Beadery
PO Box 460
Rollinsville, CO 80474
(303) 258-9389
www.beyondbeadery.com

Blue Moon Beads
www.bluemoonbeads.com
7855 Hayvenhurst Avenue
Van Nuys, CA 91406

Bobby Bead
2831 Hennepin Ave. South
Minneapolis, MN 55408
(612) 879-8181
www.bobbybead.com

Bokamo Designs
5609 W. 99th St.
Overland Park, KS 66207
(913) 648-4296
www.bokamodesigns.com

Bonnie's Beads
2708A W. Colorado Ave.
Colorado Springs, CO 80904
(719) 477-1919
www.bonniesbeads.com

Caravan Beads
915 Forest Ave.
Portland, ME 04103
(800) 230-8941
www.caravanbeads.com

CF Originals
Christi Friesen
PO Box 944
Tehachapi, CA 93581
(661) 822-6999
www.cforiginals.com

Charm Factory
(866) 867-5266
www.charmfactory.com

Chevron Trading Post & Bead Co.
(800) 881-2323
www.chevronbeads.com

Cindybeads
11734 W. 76th Ln.
Arvada, CO 80005
(303) 423-1616
www.cindybeads.com

Clay River Designs
303-849-5234
www.clayriverdesigns.com

Gail Crosman Moore
(978) 575-0790
www.gailcrosmanmoore.com

Da Beads
(708) 606-6542
www.dabeads.com

DACS Beads
1287 Kalani St. #102
Honolulu, HI 96817
(808) 842-7714
www.dacsbeads.com

Dakota Enterprises
(wholesale only)
7279 Washington Ave. South
Edina, MN 55439
(612) 298-7371
www.dakotastones.com

Dallas Designs
Vilma Dallas
(303) 469-1968

Dante Amor
Shifting Sands Studios
1337 Hoapili St.
Lahaina, HI 96761
(808) 573-2479

David Christensen
215 Shady Lea Rd., Ste. 102
North Kingstown, RI 02852
(401) 294-1440
ceneglass@hotmail.com

Desert Gems
457 Wadsworth
Lakewood, CO 80226
(303) 426-4411
www.desertgemsinc.com

Jack Dewitt
Eagle Beads, 317
Mid Valley Shopping Center
Carvel Valley, CA 93923
(408) 626-3575

Dragon Art Inc.
(877) 388-8228
www.dragonartinc.com

Dyed in the Fire Designs
PO Box 1659
Mars Hill, NC 28754
(828) 689-8934
plcahill@aol.com

Eclectica
www.eclecticabeads.com

Eebeads.com
www.eebeads.com

Family Glass
www.familyglass.com

FineDings.com
www.finedings.com

Fire in Belly
275 Jack Youce Rd.
Guffey, CO 80820
(719) 689-2388

**Fire Mountain
Gems and Beads**
www.firemountaingems.com

Fusion Beads
3830 Stone Wy. N
Seattle, WA 98103
(888) 781-3559
www.fusionbeads.com

**Gems Resources
Enterprise**
(wholesale only)
339 5th Ave. 3rd Fl.
New York, NY 10016
(800) 992-8483
www.gemresources.com

General Bead
317 National City Blvd.
National City, CA 91950-1110
(619) 336-0100
www.genbead.com

Glass Galore
6556 SW Alden Street
Portland, OR 97223
(503) 246-7199
www.glassgalore.com

**Glorianna's Fine Crafts,
Inc.**
55 West Marcy Street
Santa Fe, NM 87501
(505) 982-0353

Green Girl Studios
PO Box 19389
Asheville, NC 28815
877-GGSTUDIOS
www.greengirlstudios.com

Harold Williams Cooney
PO Box 810
Boulder, CO 80306
(303) 545-2230
www.glassartists.org/
HaroldWilliamsCooney

I Dream of Beading
488 Freedom Plains Rd, #107
Freedom Executive Park
Poughkeepsie, NY 12603
(845) 452-7611
www.idreamofbeading.com

Imagine That!
www.imaginebeads.com

Jane's Fiber and Beads
(423) 639-7919 or
(888) 497-2665
www.janesfiberandbeads.com

Jess Imports
66 Gough St.
San Francisco, CA 94102
(415) 626-1433
www.jessimports.com

Jiley's Studio
Jiley Romney
www.jileysstudio.com

John Winter
WinterGlas
12009 Devilwood Dr.
Potomac, MD 20854
www.winterglas.com

Joyce Rooks
(760) 492-3805
www.joycerooks.com

**Just Enough by Cousin
Corporation**
www.cousin.com
(727) 536-3568

Kamol
(wholesale only)
PO Box 95619
Seattle, WA 98145
(206) 764-7375
kamolbeads@yahoo.com

Kate McKinnon
ww.katemckinnon.com

Kim Miles
www.kimmiles.com

Kipuka Trading
(808) 298-3208
www.kipukatrading.com

Knot Just Beads
515 Glenview Ave.
Wauwatosa, WI 53213
(414) 771-8360
www.knotjustbeads.com

**Kristal Wick Creations/
Sassy Silkies**
(866) 811-1376
www.kristalwick.com

Lewis Wilson
Crystal Myths
(505) 883-9295
www.crystalmyths.com

Lillypilly Designs
www.lillypillydesigns.com

Loco Lobo Designs
Janis Holler
5821 WCR 8E
Berthoud, CO 80513
www.locolobodesigns.com

Loveland Bead Company
2022 W. Eisenhower
Loveland, CO 80538
(970) 667-4092

Lucky Gems and Jewelry
(wholesale only)
1220 Broadway, 3/F
New York, NY 10001
(212) 268-8866
www.lucky-gems.com

Marsha Neal Studio
www.marshanealstudio.com

MB Imports
(206) 374 9042
www.mbbeads.com

Michaels
www.michaels.com

Michele McManus
(303) 394-9033
www.michelemcmanus.com

Jennifer Morris
(213) 250-0040
jenn.morris@sbcglobal.net

Michael Barley
2003 Kuhn St.
Port Townsend, WA 98368
(360) 385-3064
www.barleybeads.com

The Moontide Workshop
38 W. Branchville Rd.
Ridgefield, CT 06877
(203) 544-8330
www.moontideworkshop.com

Mother Beads
152 Legend Oaks Wy.
Summerville, SC 29485
(943) 851-1641
www.motherbeads.com

Natural Touch Beads
PO Box 2713
Petaluma, CA 94953
(707) 781-0808
www.naturaltouchbeads.com

**New Mexico Bead and
Fetish**
401 Romero St. NW, Old Town
Albuquerque, NM 87104.
www.nmbeadandfetish.com

Nancy Tobey
www.nancytobey.com

Nina Designs
(wholesale only)
PO Box 8127
Emeryville, CA 94662
(800) 336-6462
www.ninadesigns.com

Orr's Trading Company
3422 S. Broadway
Englewood, CO 80110
(303) 722-6466
www.orrs.com

Oskadusa
243 North Highway 101
Solana Beach, CA 92075
(858) 755-2323
www.oskadusa.com

Pacific Silverworks
461 E. Main St., Ste. 1-A
Ventura, CA 93001
(805) 641-1394
www.pacificsilverworks.com

Paula Radke
PO Box 1088
Morro Bay, CA 93443
(800) 341-4945
www.paularadke.com

Pema Arts
1761 Walnut St.
El Cerrito, CA 94530
(510) 965-9956
www.tibetanbeads.com

Promenade le Bead Shop
1970 13th St.
Boulder, CO 80302
(303) 440-4807

Pudgy Beads
1150 E. Wardlow Rd.
Long Beach, CA 90807
(562) 427-0018
www.pudgybeads.com

Random Acts of Clay
www.randomacts.150m.com

Raven's Journey
PO Box 3099
Port Angeles, WA 98362
(206) 406-7491
www.theravenstore.com

Redside Designs
175 Adams St.
Eugene, OR 97402
www.redsidedesigns.net

Rejiquar Works
www.rejiquar.com

Rings & Things
PO Box 450
Spokane, WA 99210-0450
(800) 366-2156
www.rings-things.com

Rio Grande
7500 Bluewater Rd. Northwest
Albuquerque, NM 87121
(800) 545-6566
www.riogrande.com

Rishashay
(800) 517-3311
www.rishashay.com

Saki Silver
362 Ludlow Ave.
Cincinnati, OH 45220
(513) 861-9626
www.sakisilver.com

Scottsdale Bead Supply
3625 N. Marshall Wy.
Scottsdale, AZ 85251-5515
(480) 945-5988
www.scottsdalebead.com

Shoba
5645 Hillcroft Avenue, #502
Houston, TX 77036-2241
(713) 781-5152

Singaraja Imports
www.singarajaimports.com

Soft Flex Company
PO Box 89
Sonoma, CA 95476
(707) 938-3539
www.softflexcompany.com

Sojourner
(609) 397-8849
www.sojourner.biz

Some Enchanted Beading
2 North Main St.
Willsboro, NY 12996
www.someenchanted
beading.com

Somerset Silver
(wholesale only)
PO Box 5546
Bellevue, WA 98006
(425) 641-3666
www.somerset-silver.com

Springall Adventures
HC70 Box 9A
Glorieta, NM 87535
(505) 757-6520

Star Mountain Trading
409 Bullard
Silver City, NM 88061
(888) 782-7686
www.strmtntrading.com

Star's Clasps
139A Church St. Northwest
Vienna, VA 22180
(800) 207-2805
www.starsclasps.com

Stone Mountain Bead Gallery
3100 Central Ave. Southeast
Albuquerque, NM 87106
(505) 260-1121

Suze!
3823 Tamiami Trl. E PMB #512
Naples, FL 34112
(239) 775-9859

Sweet Creek Creations
(541) 997-0109
www.sweetcreek.com

Ta Pearlstone
1044 Grant Ave. #123
San Francisco, CA 94133
(415) 505-9148
www.tapearlstone.com

Talisman Associates
2001-A Veirs Mill Rd.
Rockville, MD 20851
(800) 229-7890
www.talismanbeads.com

Tamara Honaman
(610) 564-0826
tamara_honaman@comcast.net

Thunderbird Supply Company
1907 W. Historic Rte. 66
Gallup, NM 87301
(800) 545-7968
www.thunderbirdsupply.com

TierraCast
(wholesale only)
3177 Guerneville Rd.
Santa Rose, CA 94501
(800) 222-9939
www.tierracast.com

Tom Simpson
PO Box 1598
Guerneville, CA 95446
(707) 865-4132

Two Cranes
Box 116
Socorro, NM 87801
(505) 835-9225
www.2cranes.biz

Via Murano
PO Box 10081
Newport Beach, CA 92658
(877) VIA-MURANO
www.viamurano.com

Whitney Street Studio
www.whitneystreetstudio.com

Wild Things
Pine Grove, CA 95665
(209) 296-8447
www.wildthingsbeads.com

Wildfire Designs
www.wildfire-designs.com

WinterGlas
12009 Devilwood Drive
Potomac, MD 20854-3414
www.winterglas.com

Worldly Goods
PO Box 250
Ashland, OR 97520
(541) 488-7881
www.wordlygoods
buttons.com

Zeka Beads
12400 State Hwy. 71 West
Ste. 350, Box 196
Austin, TX 78738
(512) 264-3054
www.zekabeads.com

ZnetShows
(866) 824-1832
www.znetshows.com

Zoa Art
1927 Floyd Blackwell Rd.
Tryon, NC 28782
(864) 680-7541
www.zoaart.com

BRACELET BONANZA (p. 20)

Unless otherwise noted, the materials used in the earrings were from the designer's own collection.

1. Designed by Ruby Bayan. All materials: Imagine That! 2. Designed by Carol Reesha. Clasp, spacers, and peace charm: Sadco, Inc; crystals: Beads U Need. 3. Designed by Karen Wood. Wood: The Bead Hut; pearls: Lucky Gems & Jewelry (wholesale only). 4. Designed by Terry Ricioli. Turquoise and silver: New Mexico Bead and Fetish; glass: Blue Moon Beads. 5. Designed by Paulette Livers. Clasp: Jess Imports; artistic stone drop: Dakota Enterprises; Peruvian opals: Sweet Creek Creations; polished turquoise: Two Cranes; Czech pressed-glass beads: Applegate Lapidary. 6. Designed by Gail Kanemoto Hogsett. India glass: The Bead Goes On; Czech glass: Fusion Beads; spacers and clasp: TierraCast (wholesale only). 7. Designed by Cynthia Thornton. Seashell clasp, head bead, small eye rock: Green Girl Studios; wooden alchemy bead: Lillypilly Designs; labradorite, ruby, quartz, kyanite, abalone/resin, and tourmaline: MB Imports; silver spacers: Kamol (wholesale only). 8. Designed by Cynthia Thornton. Large mermaid button and seahorse dangle: Green Girl Studios; tourmaline: Chevron Trading Post & Bead Co.; silver spacers: Kamol (wholesale only). 9. Designed by Bonnie Gorton. Purple turquoise: Dakota Enterprises; silver bead caps: Ands Silver; Czech glass and crystals: Beyond Beadery. 10. Designed by Wendy Bialek. Raku: Random Acts of Clay; purple shells: Eclectica; crystal: Bead Boss; clasp: FineDings.com. 11. Designed by Laura Levaas. Clasp: Kipuka Trading. 12. Designed by Bonnie Gorton. Clasp: Rishashay; pearls, crystals, and seed beads: Bead Cache. 13. Designed by Bonnie Gorton. Clasp and seed beads: Beyond Beadery; foil glass: Michaels; 2-strand spacer bar: Bead Cache. 14. Designed by Laura Levaas. Crystals: Beyond Beadery; clasp, mirrored beads, and crystals: Pudgy Beads. 15. Designed by Jenna Coylar-Cooper. All materials: Fusion Beads. 16. Designed by Danielle Fox. Glass beads: Gems Resources Enterprise (wholesale only); curved silver tubes: Somerset Silver (wholesale only); spacers: Bead Cache; clasp: Saki Silver. 17. Designed by Marlene Blessing. Mother-of-pearl beads: Soft Flex Company; marcasite, silver beads, and toggle clasp: Nina Designs (wholesale only). 18. Designed by Bonnie Gorton. Toggle, jasper, lampwork, and pearls: Bead Cache; crystals: Beyond Beadery. 19. Designed by Ruby Bayan. All materials: Bead Time. 20. Designed by Ruby Bayan. All materials: Bead Time. 21. Designed by Carol Reesha. Clasp: Sadco; Glass and pearls: Oskadusa. 22. Designed by Regina Greer-Smith. All materials: Michaels. 23. Designed by Rebecca Campbell. Vintage lucite: Fusion Beads; clasp: Sojourner. 24. Designed by Laura Levaas. Clasp and black disks: Pudgy Beads; crystal rondelles: Beyond Beadery. 25. Designed by Ruby Bayan. All materials: Bead Bar. 26. Designed by Gail Kanemoto Hogsett. Coral: Glorianna's; silver rounds: Singaraja Imports; onyx: Dakota Enterprises; clasp: Saki Silver. 27. Designed by Jamie Hogsett. Clasp: Somerset Silver (wholesale only); spacers: Saki Silver; briolettes: Fusion Beads. 28. Designed by Danielle Fox. Czech pressed-glass and fire-polished beads: Raven's Journey; corrugated silver beads and spacers: Desert Gems; clasp: Nina Designs (wholesale only). 29. Designed by Julie Wood. Clasp: Sojourner. 30. Designed by Kerry Flint. Fire-polished beads: Jack Dewitt; vintage Czech glass beads: Talisman Associates 31. Designed by Kerry Flint. Fire-polished beads: Jack Dewitt; glass beads: Glass Galore; green turquoise: Beadstringers; clasp: Bokamo Designs. 32. Designed by Kerry Flint. Silver spacers: Bead Cache; green turquoise: Beadstringers. 33. Designed by Jamie Hogsett. India glass and spacers: The Bead Goes On; crystals: Beyond Beadery; clasp: Saki Silver. 34. Designed by Julie Wood. Millefiori: Better Creation; clasp: The Bead Goes On. 35. Designed by Marlene Blessing. Blue and green Czech glass beads: Raven's Journey; silver hand pendant: Pacific Silverworks; stamped silver cylinder beads: Nina Designs (wholesale only); twisted silver toggle clasp: Fusion Beads. 36. Designed by Dustin Wedekind. Clasp: Saki Silver; vintage glass and porcelain beads: Bead Cache. 37. Designed by Marlene Blessing. Glass lozenges: Raven's Journey; stamped silver cube and silver dangles: Somerset Silver (wholesale only); clasp: Saki Silver. 38. Designed by Cynthia Thornton. Branch toggle and sun rock: Green Girl Studios; fire opals: MB Imports; silver spacers: Kamol (wholesale only). 39. Designed by Regina Greer-Smith. Citrine and pearls: Lucky Gems & Jewelry (wholesale only). 40. Designed by Kerry Flint. Glass beads: Glass Galore; crystals: Beyond Beadery; coin resin beads: eebeads.com. 41. Designed by Regina Greer-Smith. All Beads: Fire Mountain Gems and Beads. 42. Designed by Marlene Blessing. Lampworked focal beads: WinterGlas; lampworked spacer beads: Jane's Fiber and Beads; clasp: Saki Silver. 43. Designed by Marlene Blessing. Pearls: Lucky Gems & Jewelry (wholesale only); stamped silver cubes: The Bead Goes On; silver stones: Somerset Silver (wholesale only); clasp: Pacific Silverworks. 44. Designed by Karen Wood. Glass rounds: Loveland Bead Company; spacers and clasp: The Bead Goes On; stone: Dakota Enterprises. 45. Designed by Annie Bakken. Moukite: Gems Resources Enterprise; clasp: Somerset Silver (wholesale only). 46. Designed by Marlene Blessing. Czech glass beads: Raven's Journey; clasp: Singaraja Imports. 47. Designed by Dustin Wedekind. Clasp: TierraCast (wholesale only). 48. Designed by Gail Kanemoto Hogsett. Clasp: Sojourner.

EARRINGS EUPHORIA (p. 24)

Unless otherwise noted, the materials used in the earrings were from the designer's own collection.

1. Designed by Rebecca Campbell. All materials: Bead Cache. 2. Czech glass flowers: Raven's Journey; silver charms: TierraCast (wholesale only). 3. Designed by Danielle Fox. Corrugated silver barrels: Desert Gems; Czech pressed glass: Raven's Journey. 4. Czech pressed glass: Raven's Journey; crystals: Fusion Beads. 5. Designed by Keriann Gore. All materials: Bead Cache. 6. Designed by Dustin Wedekind. Vintage white crystal flowers: Beyond Beadery. 7. Designed by Keriann Gore. All materials: Bead Cache. 8. Murano glass beads: Via Murano. 9. Designed by Keriann Gore. All materials: Bead Cache. 10. Designed by Danielle Fox. Dichroic charms: Paula Radke Dichroic Glass. 11. Czech pressed glass: Bokamo Designs; gold spacers: TierraCast (wholesale only). 12. Lampworked beads: Whitney Street Studio; silver hoops: Fusion Beads. 13. Chain: House of Gems; crystals: Beyond Beadery. 14. Pewter charms: Green Girl Studios; red wire: Beadalon (wholesale only). 15. Etched stones and vintage lucite beads: The Moontide Workshop. 16. Designed by Keriann Gore. All materials: Bead Cache. 17. Pewter fish beads: Green Girl Studios; crystals: Fusion Beads. 18. Designed by Lindsay Burke. All materials: Fusion Beads. 19. Lampworked beads: Whitney Street Studio; earring posts: Nina Designs (wholesale only); crystals: Fusion Beads. 20. Swarovski crystals: Bead-time. 21. Designed by Sara Hardin. All materials: Soft Flex Company. 22. Brazilian beads: Jane's Fiber and Beads. 23. Designed by Keriann Gore. All materials: Bead Cache. 24. Designed by Paulette Livers. Cane glass: David Christensen. 25. Borosilicate glass: Family Glass; crystals: Beyond Beadery. 26. Designed by Dustin Wedekind. Bead caps: TierraCast (wholesale only). 27. Purple turquoise: Dakota Enterprises (wholesale only); charms: TierraCast (wholesale only). 28. Designed by Danielle Fox. Ear wires: Nina Designs (wholesale only). 29. Bead caps: TierraCast (wholesale only); Swarovski pearls: Fusion Beads. 30. Emeralds: Bead-time; soldered jump rings: Fusion Beads. 31. Thai silver triangle beads: Somerset Silver (wholesale only). 32. Thai silver crescent beads: Saki Silver; soldered jump rings: Fusion Beads. 33. Bali silver hoops: Nina Designs (wholesale only); Swarovski pearls: Fusion Beads. 34. Pink cubic zirconias: MB Imports. 35. Designed by Danielle Fox. Glass cubes: Bead Cache; Czech pressed glass: Raven's Journey; pineapple quartz: Desert Gems. 36. Lampworked beads: Cindybeads; silver beads: Bob Burkett through Green Girl Studios. 37. Designed by Julie Wood. Glass beads: Fire Mountain Gems and Beads. 38. Designed by Lindsay Burke. All materials: Fusion Beads. 39. Silk beads: Sassy Silkies; dichroic glass: Paula Radke Dichroic Glass. 40. Designed by Danielle Fox. Red pressed glass disks: Bokomo Designs. 41. Designed by Carol Reesha. Glass and pearls: Dragon Art; crystals: Beads U Need. 42. Designed by Julie Wood. Chandelier findings: Fusion Beads. 43. Designed by Maha Rizk. All materials: Bead Club. 44. Turquoise, pearls, and chandelier pieces: Fusion Beads. 45. Clay beads: Clay River Designs; crystals: Fusion Beads. 46. Ear findings: Fusion Beads; crystals: Beyond Beadery. 47. Czech glass flowers: Raven's Journey; crystals: Fusion Beads; clay beads: Clay River Designs. 48. Rubies: Soft Flex Company; silver: Saki Silver. 49. Designed by Beth Simmons. Czech glass ovals and leaves: I Dream of Beading. 50. Vintage lucite: Gail Crosman Moore; ceramic beads: Marsha Neal Studio. 51. Vintage lucite: Gail Crosman Moore; silver: Somerset Silver (wholesale only). 52. Designed by Annie Bakken. Moukite: Gems Resources Enterprise 53. Millefiori: Better Creation; ear findings: Saki Silver. 54. Ear hoops: Beads and Beyond; crystals: Fusion Beads; silver: Kamol (wholesale only). 55. Crystals and chandelier pieces: Fusion Beads. 56. Designed by Kristal Wick. Sassy Silkies silk beads and silver disks: Kristal Wick Creations; Swarovski crystals and findings: Rings & Things. 57. Crystals and rhinestone beads: Fusion Beads. 58. Crystals: Fusion Beads; Silver tubes: TierraCast (wholesale only). 59. Crystals and diamond chain: Fusion Beads. 60. Hoops and crystals: Fusion Beads; clay beads: Clay River Designs. 61. Designed by Danielle Fox. Silver flowers: Somerset Silver (wholesale only); rondelles: Raven's Journey; ear wires: Nina Designs (wholesale only). 62. Designed by Ruby Bayan. Millefiori: ZnetShows; Snake chain: Charm Factory. 63. Design by Kristal Wick. All materials: Kristal Wick Creations. 64. Designed by Regina Greer-Smith. Blue-lace agate: Shoba 65. Designed by Danielle Fox. Raku beads: Fire in Belly; ear wires, chain, and head pins: Fusion Beads. 66. Designed by Beth Simmons. Czech glass ovals and leaves: I Dream of Beading. 67. Designed by Katie Wall. All materials: Fusion Beads. 68. Designed by Keriann Gore. All materials: Bead Cache. 69. Aqua drops: Lucky Gems & Jewelry (wholesale only); chain: Fusion Beads. 70. Tulips: Beads and Beyond; chain: Fusion Beads. 71. Designed by Danielle Fox. Purple glass tabs: Da Beads; fire-polished beads: Raven's Journey; chain, wire, and ear wires: Fusion Beads. 72. Designed by Danielle Fox. Polymer earring bases: Jennifer Morrison; gold chain, head pins, and ear wires: Fusion Beads; fire-polished beads: Raven's Journey. 73. Fish: Beads and Beyond; chain, hoops, and crystals: Fusion Beads. 74. Crystals: Fusion Beads; silver floral beads: Nina Designs (wholesale only). 75. Designed by Terry Ricioli. Filigree: Just Enough by Cousin Corporation; glass: Blue Moon Beads. 76. Designed by Karen Wood. Jewelry cable wire: Beadalon (wholesale only); Czech pressed-glass: Raven's Journey.

Index